FROM
Clergy to Convert

From
Clergy to
Convert

COMPILED BY
Stephen W. Gibson

Bookcraft
Salt Lake City, Utah

Library of Congress Catalog Card Number: 83-71802
ISBN 0-88494-492-1

2 3 4 5 6 7 8 9 10   89 88 87 86 85 84 83

Lithographed in the United States of America
PUBLISHERS PRESS
Salt Lake City, Utah

Contents

Preface vii

What Will Become of Me?
John Herring 1

The Lord Knew That I Knew
Judith Svoboda 9

How Do I Get Into This Outfit?
Carr Krueger 16

Daddy, What Have You Done?
John Harber 23

I Didn't Want to Change
John Reiher 31

I Was Just Simply Curious
Norman Carlisle 40

I Knew I Was Their Target
Frank Tapp 47

What If . . . ?
Ralph Drake 55

I Felt I Was Saved
Ronald Palmer 61

We Waited for Six Years
William and Alexandria Schnoebelen 67

A Case of Mistaken Identity
James D. Morask 74

It Felt As If We Had Come Home
Mary Jane Reed 82

I Wanted Him Perfect
Norman Knight 92

Three Questions Haunted Me
Patrick McGee 98

Preface

In 1971, as a photojournalist for the *Church News*, I flew to southern California to interview a man who had been miraculously healed at the water's edge after being baptized. When I arrived I learned that this man, James Morask, was a Baptist minister for twenty-two years and had given up that ministry to join The Church of Jesus Christ of Latter-day Saints.

His conversion story intrigued me so much that I started a ten-year project of locating ministers, nuns, priests, and rabbis who have received the restored gospel. The research has been thrilling to me as I have located more than a hundred in that category. They are currently serving the Lord in callings ranging from class teacher to Regional Representative.

As I have interviewed these men and women, I have been impressed with three common threads in their conversion stories:

1. Often a main factor in conversion has been their intimate knowledge of the Bible coupled with a comparison of the New Testament Church and the LDS Church of today. Making that comparison required that they first open their minds to the possibility of a latter-day prophet. Once they did that, exciting things began to happen.

2. Two young men or women missionaries have been instrumental in nearly every conversion. Although not trained in divinity schools, by bearing humble testimony they have influenced men and women with theological degrees and honors to offer prayers "with real intent" and to find their answers in the restored gospel.

3. Repeatedly I have found evidence of what I call the "multiple-exposure concept." That is, most of these converts met different missionaries or other Mormons several times in various locales prior to their serious investigation of LDS teachings. In other words, while initially they weren't interested, later contacts with Mormons and changes in their own situations prompted

investigation of LDS doctrines. For Latter-day Saints the moral is clear: We may not always see the harvest, but we should plant the seed anyway.

Through these stories the reader will gain these and other insights into missionary work and the conversion process.

I express appreciation to the many who over the years have helped me with this book. Current and former mission presidents have assisted by telling me of converts. John Herring, former United Methodist minister, and his wife, Pat, have been most helpful in spurring me to renew my dedication to the book after the project had lain dormant for years.

I especially appreciate the response of those whose sacred conversion stories are contained within these pages. Their courage and faith in the first place and then their permission to tell these stories to the world have made possible a book which has been an inspiration to me in the compiling, and which I believe will have a similar effect on all who read it.

What Will Become of Me?

*To trade a career of standing behind a pulpit for a job work-
ing behind prison bars doesn't sound like a good deal, but
then neither does moving from a beautifully furnished
parsonage to a small, poorly heated log cabin. Yet the
Herring family would do it all again, if that were the price
they had to pay to find eternal joy. They now know the
answer to their nagging question, "What Will Become of
Me?" as they live and work in the Denver area of Colorado.*

*N*o one likes to make changes, and my wife, Pat, and I are
no different. But when you feel a call from the Lord, you sometimes have to change things regardless of the obstacles and
discomforts.

This was certainly the case when our family was young. I was
following a successful career in banking, serving as executive
officer of a small bank in West Virginia, when I felt a strong urge
to enter the ministry—no matter what the personal sacrifices.
Seven years of college training lay ahead of me, and without the
willing support of my wife and four children, such an effort
would have been foolish.

To my surprise, my wife was thrilled, rather than upset, by
my decision. It seemed to her that this was the will of God. We
immediately listed our home for sale, and although we were told
it was unmarketable, we sold it within three weeks.

At Averett College in Virginia I pushed through the four-year program in only three years with the help of my family—and made the Dean's list each year. Upon graduation I affiliated with the United Methodist Church as pastor of four little mountain congregations in the Blue Ridge. The salary and the parsonage were very enticing, particularly because I wanted to further my theological education at Duke University, which has one of the finest divinity schools anywhere. It would be no small thing to be admitted there, so I was thrilled when I received my letter of acceptance along with a full scholarship grant. Pat and I felt unbelievably blessed by the Lord.

Soon I was driving two hundred miles a day round trip to Duke University, leaving at 5:00 A.M. and returning around 6:00 P.M. to make hospital visits and do other church work. My congregations were dissatisfied with this arrangement: they felt they should get a full-time minister for the salary they were paying. Nonetheless, the fifteen-hour-a-day struggle continued for three years.

But as the time for my graduation from Duke approached, I found myself sinking into great despair. My classes had stressed the importance of understanding God by personal experience and not borrowing theology from other people. I had diligently pursued this personal relationship with God, yet when I stood back to take inventory of my beliefs—of who I was and where I was—I realized the bitter truth: I did not belong in the United Methodist Church. Nor did I belong in the Baptist Church I had grown up in. In fact, my study showed me I did not belong anywhere.

My beliefs seemed pretty radical. I was offended at the idea that the holy scriptures were considered finished, that inspired words would never again be written. I remember the serious problem I had in trying to understand the doctrine of Holy Trinity. When I went to one of my professors to get an explanation, he referred me to a library floor where I would find untold numbers of books trying to explain that doctrine.

I'll never forget another professor I approached with this question: "I know that every Protestant and Catholic church believes in the doctrine of the Trinity, but I simply cannot believe it. What am I to do? Am I to consider myself blasphemous? Am I to write off all these years of education and quit because I can't buy this point of theology?" He laughed a little and said, "I can't believe it myself." He told me that everyone encounters these impasses but that our value in the ministry must come from other sources. We went on to discuss how strange it was to visualize Jesus praying to himself and answering his own prayers.

I was also put off by such teachings as infant baptism and confirmation at age twelve—I had a lot of problems. But here I was, getting older, with seven years invested in an education of little value in the business world. I knew I was stuck trapped. The Methodist Church provides so much for its ministers: a home, furniture, even pots and pans, silverware, glasses, and sheets. We were well kept—and I emphasize "kept." I also felt strange being paid to visit the sick and share the gospel with others. When the treasurer would hand me my paycheck, I would ask myself why I was being paid to do just what I was telling others to do.

I became physically ill over these feelings. My congregations discouraged me, too. Many influential people were disturbed because I insisted on preaching to everyone—not just the white folks—and I remember clearly the threats of the Ku Klux Klan against my family. My congregations believed their salvation was indeed secure just by virtue of walking into the church once a week. I remember feeling I was preaching to the brick walls.

One evening, in total despair, Pat and I went to our room and fell to our knees, weeping bitterly. I cried out to my Heavenly Father, "Dear God, if there is a place for me, if there is really a church where Jesus Christ can be found, please let me know now." I knew then that I had to leave the ministry, though I feared what would become of me.

The following Sunday morning was terrible. I stood at the

pulpit and preached things I really felt—things Methodists have no use for. I can remember the bitter, puzzled looks on the faces of the few who were listening. I was sure that within days I would be asked to leave.

That evening a knock came at the door. There on our doorstep stood a young man, his wife, and two children. They introduced themselves as John and Joyce Harber and asked if they could come in. John said, "We have been visiting with my wife's parents, who are members of your church, and have heard many things about your beliefs. We felt we should visit you because we believe these things too." Upon driving out of town, he had felt an uncontrollable urge to pull in my driveway and call on us.

I was amazed when he told us he too had been a Methodist minister but had left that church to join The Church of Jesus Christ of Latter-day Saints. I'll never forget when he looked straight in my eyes and said, "With every fiber of my being, I know this is the only true church on the face of the earth." Chills ran over me, but I could not believe my ears. I had always thought of Mormons as ridiculous—even stupid. A paper on Mormonism I had written in college dredged up every bit of dirt and half-truth I could find—and believe me, there was a lot.

Before the Harbers left, however, I agreed reluctantly to listen to the LDS missionaries. When the missionaries came, I was thrilled with the things they told us; but when I got on my knees to tell the Lord I would leave the ministry, I knew I couldn't afford to leave. I had seven years invested in my education as a minister, and a minister I must be.

Furthermore, the church transferred me to a very enticing place, to a large Washington, D.C., suburb in Northern Virginia. The church there had a large congregation of two thousand with five staff members. I couldn't turn it down.

Once settled in, we "escaped" to our little log cabin on the Potomac River that we had purchased some months earlier. And while we were "getting away from it all," the missionaries found us again. One night after the Elders had left following another lesson, my wife pulled up a chair and said: "You know I love you, that I would not want to hurt you—but I want to ask you something. Would you be too hurt if I were to be baptized into The Church of Jesus Christ of Latter-day Saints? I feel this is the answer to our prayers; and though I know you fear you can't, I do want to be baptized. Please tell me how you feel."

My wife and I have always had a beautiful relationship, and even though I could see the problems this would cause, my response was, "If this is what you feel is right, then you must do it." Once her baptism was arranged, she asked if I would go with her, but I said I just couldn't do that. With that, she drove for two and a half hours to the Richmond Virginia Stake Center and was baptized a member of The Church of Jesus Christ of Latter-day Saints.

A Methodist minister with a Mormon wife is not exactly good public relations. We had a long talk and decided to keep her baptism confidential. She went to church with me for our early service and then drove across town to the Woodbridge Ward, maintaining a "low profile." But I should have realized she could not remain an anonymous Latter-day Saint for long. During her first week she revealed "our secret" to the Relief Society president. I was very angry when Pat said she had told this woman. *This is it*, I thought. *These Mormons are going to beat me over the head with this.* I could almost see the headlines: "Rev. Herring's Wife Joins Mormon Church." I will never be able to forgive myself for the things I said to Pat that night, accusing her of betraying me.

Then I was furious when she told me the Relief Society president, this "crazy old Mormon lady," was coming by on Thursday night to visit! I made absolutely sure not to be home when she came, but after I thought it was safe to return I found her still there, sitting on my couch. When I came in, she gave me a loving, understanding smile which my hardened heart mistook as obnoxious. As soon as the woman had left, Pat told me we were invited to her home for dinner to meet some friends. I ranted and raved that I would never, under any circumstances, go with her. I was in enough trouble as it was—our livelihood was already at stake!

After I calmed down a few days later, Pat again asked me to go and enjoy it without making such a big thing out of it. Reluctantly I agreed. That evening we met Feltus Sterling and his wife, Ruth Ann, who were very charming people. When I found out he was an FBI agent, and that our host, Fred Richardson, was a navy commander, I realized that Mormons were a long way from being the dummies I had expected. Even Nancy, Fred's wife (whom I still call that "crazy old Mormon lady"), was very pleasant.

The evening was delightful. No phoniness—just open and honest conversation, without a word about Mormonism or my church. When it was after 10:00 P.M., I looked over at Feltus Sterling and said: "You know, I'm a little disappointed. I really came over here expecting a debate, and I don't see it happening." With that, he reared back and said, "Well now, brother, since you mention it. . . ." Thus began the most liberating conversation I've ever had. When I left that evening I knew in my heart that I had been a Mormon for many years without knowing it. I cannot overemphasize, however, how great my fear was. What would become of me if I were to leave the Methodist ministry? How would we survive?

So I didn't do anything. I ignored the prompting of the Spirit entirely. I sold out for money and remained in the ministry.

Then in December I became very ill—the doctor called it bronchial pneumonia and insisted I stay in bed at least a week to get better. While lying there with nothing else to do, I picked up the Triple Combination—the Book of Mormon, the Doctrine and Covenants, and the Pearl of Great Price. From cover to cover I went, trying to find things to complain about, but the Spirit overwhelmed me and I could find nothing wrong with any of the books. A book on Church history someone had given my wife helped me as I read the Doctrine and Covenants. When I finished I had a testimony that Joseph Smith was a prophet and no fraud.

Two doctrinal obstacles had stood in my path. One was dissolved when President Spencer W. Kimball announced that Blacks could receive the priesthood. The other was accepting Joseph Smith as a prophet, and now this was out of the way. Now I too had a testimony; not from empirical knowledge but from the witness of the Spirit.

I stayed in bed Sunday, though I felt well enough. I just didn't want to live the lie in my heart anymore, so I waited until Sunday evening to tell my wife I was going to be baptized.

Monday morning I went into the office of my church, packed a few of my personal belongings, and said my good-byes. I have never returned.

On December 23, 1978, I entered the waters of baptism at the hands of Elder Jay Scow, whose family I have come to know as an inspiration of patience, persistence, preparedness, and love.

After my baptism, the people of Woodbridge Ward and R. C. Powell, the branch president from the area to which we were moving, came in their vans and cars and loaded up everything we owned to drive the eighty miles to our little log cabin. We set up housekeeping with no central heat, cutting many a cord of wood alongside Brother Powell to keep our stove going. I remained unemployed through January and February, and our only food came to our doorstep from members of the little branch in Tappahannock.

After two months I went to work at unit 17 of the Virginia State Penitentiary at one-fourth as much as my salary as a minister. Four years later not much has changed, although we have moved to Colorado, where I am general manager of a small petroleum company. Things are still tight financially, but we have a joy in our lives that few people understand, and we are making great strides toward normalization of our temporal lives. We are at peace with each other and our Heavenly Father. We have returned to him in this life, which is the greatest of all blessings. Even though we took a financial dive, the windows of heaven are being opened up to us and we feel surrounded by love and truth. Our oldest son, John Jr., is now serving in the Finland Helsinki Mission, and our daughter Debbie is in Ecuador on her mission. Our two other sons are now saving money and preparing for their missions.

All this I owe to our Heavenly Father, whose Spirit bears witness that we are in the true church of Jesus Christ. We have a prophet leading the Church today, for whom I have great love and respect. I bear this testimony to those who may be seeking the truth—do not make the mistake of presupposing where you may or may not find it. Open your eyes, open your heart, and listen as you pray with all your heart. You will know it when you find it.

The Lord Knew That I Knew

It had been four years since Judith Svoboda left the convent after eighteen years as a nun. Things on the outside weren't working out as she had hoped, and she was just about ready to become a nun again. First she wanted to borrow some ideas from the LDS Church. That borrowing became permanent, and she is now serving as a ward Relief Society president in the Chicago area.

I was born of goodly parents, Ruben Frank Swoboda and Margaret Agnes Turczynski, on August 13, 1939, at Two Rivers, Wisconsin. From my birth I was reared in the Catholic faith and taught by my good parents and the nuns at the Catholic grade school. I thrilled to the stories of Abraham, Moses, Joseph and his coat of many colors, as well as the life and ministry of Christ, his miracles and teachings. I distinctly remember my first-grade teacher speaking of the "war in heaven" and the fall of Lucifer and his angels. At the age of six I was taught that revelation from heaven had ceased with the Apostles and that "tradition" had taken its place.

Little did I know how drastically tradition had altered the original teachings of the gospel of Jesus Christ. The Bible stories impressed me much more than the catechism, with its hundreds of questions and answers on Catholic doctrine. Nevertheless, inspired by the example and love of the nuns, I left my parents' home at fourteen to join them and dedicate my life to the Lord. I entered, at Chicago, a branch of the Felician Sisters, part of the Third Order of St. Francis of Assisi.

For the next three years, as an aspirant, I attended regular classes at Good Counsel High School while living at the convent Motherhouse. A rigorous daily schedule called for morning prayer, Mass, chores, classes, study time, recreation, and evening prayer. When I think back, I feel tender gratitude in my heart for the innocence of those years and love for the sweet girls who were true sisters to me.

After graduating, I entered the novitiate as a postulant. Our daily routine differed little from the aspirancy, but now we dressed in uniform black—dresses, veils, shoes, and stockings. We had passed to the "other side," the cloistered part of the convent, and were forbidden all contact with lay persons, other than family and friends at monthly visits. The rules of the order introduced us to intense obedience and the "chapter of faults," a discipline of listing our infractions of the rule. After one year of postulancy, we took the white veil and brown habit of the order and were given a "new name." I was known as Sister Mary Blanche.

As a novice I attended theology classes in college, but most of our education dealt with the vows we would take. We were schooled in obedience, in humility, and most particularly in chastity. This vow of complete celibacy and purity in thought, desire, word, and deed did not detract from marriage and its sacredness—we were not running from something dirty, but felt we were giving up something very good in itself for something better.

Finally I took upon myself the black veil of the order and publicly professed my vows of poverty, chastity, and obedience. For the next ten years I taught, played the organ, and directed choir at parishes in Chicago and Oak Forest, Illinois; St. Paul, Minnesota; and Birmingham, Alabama.

During this period of time the Catholic Church was changing drastically. English replaced Latin in the services of the church, and lay people became more involved in the work. I was thrilled to come out of my shell and began to see more value, virtue, and sacrifice in the lives of my lay brothers and sisters than in the protected and riskless convent life. While many religious orders were allowing their sisters more freedom of choice, my own order held back, changing so cautiously that I decided to take a leave of absence for a year. I wanted to live in the world to decide whether or not I could continue in this order for the rest of my life.

I had spent eighteen years in the convent, but after two months of lay life I knew I would never return. When I received a complete dispensation from my vows from Rome, I even began to date the "male species" to determine whether or not marriage was in the Lord's plan for me. And so begins the story of my conversion to The Church of Jesus Christ of Latter-day Saints.

Upon leaving the convent, I joined a choral group where I met a man named Les Svoboda. He drove me to rehearsal every week, and it wasn't long before I came to know him for a kind, considerate, and cheerful gentleman. Often I secretly wondered if he and I would ever marry—but he had joined the Mormon Church and I knew he would never marry outside his faith. He often spoke of "eternal marriage," but I was convinced I would remain a Catholic, since I loved my church and still thought it was the true church of Christ.

Still, Les continued to tell me many good things about his church—the family home evening program, home and visiting teaching, tithing, the Word of Wisdom, and the priesthood. I remember feeling sorry for him, because I knew nothing of the Apostasy and I believed he did not have a true priesthood. I was afraid to read his strange scripture called the Book of Mormon—

it just gathered dust in my apartment. But I could see his activity in the Mormon Church had made a real difference in his life and that he was satisfied in his search for greater truth.

After four years outside the convent, working in Catholic schools as a lay teacher, I seemed not to be heading in the direction of marriage. I began to investigate a new religious order, Sisters of Christian Community, formed largely by nuns who had left stricter orders for a more active Christian life. As a member of this new order I would still live in my own apartment and continue to work in my own parish, and I wanted that freedom.

After deciding to do this, I realized that the families of our Catholic parish badly needed some spiritual help, and I decided to see Les one more time. I wanted to borrow some of those wonderful Mormon ideas for family-oriented programs. We met on Good Friday 1975 and discussed the doctrines of the Mormon Church. I found many points of comparison with Catholicism and thoroughly enjoyed the discussion. He invited me to see a Mormon play, a musical drama called "The City of Joseph," at the Westchester chapel. The play was nice, but I was even more impressed with the sweet, wholesome spirit I felt among the Mormon people—they called each other "brother" and "sister," just as we did in convent life.

After the drama, Les and his companions (he was serving as a stake missionary) came up to my apartment for a glass of orange juice. (I would have loved to offer them a whiskey sour or an old-fashioned, but I knew they didn't drink.) By the end of a two-hour discussion that evening, I had agreed to take a series of seven lessons on the Mormon beliefs. I had no intention of converting, but these men were so nice and I loved talking and praying with them. It was an offer I couldn't refuse.

Les led the first two lessons, and when he spoke of our Heavenly Father and his divine Son visiting the boy prophet Joseph Smith, I could truly believe that. It made me happy to hear that our Savior might have visited the American continent. I began to feel that I was hearing the truth, and while I interrupted a great deal at first, I found myself listening more and talking less and less. Pieces of a puzzle seemed to come together in my mind.

As I read a book called *A Marvelous Work and a Wonder*, I asked the missionaries to bring me a copy of the Doctrine and Covenants so I could look up references and hear things directly from the Prophet's mouth.

I will never forget the spell-binding effect of that book. I would come home from teaching all day and then sit in one spot for hours, drinking in those marvelous words of the Lord Jesus Christ to the Prophet Joseph. I knew the words of this book were true, and I knew the Lord knew that I knew!

By June, the Elders were meeting with me three times a week. I would read fifty pages in the Doctrine and Covenants and have questions all ready for them. I also attended sacrament meeting and the Sunday School investigators class taught by Brother D. Barney. Never had I heard anyone teach with such authority. My defenses were crumbling and the truth was pouring into my mind and heart, filling me with a joy and light I had never known. I thrilled to the plan of salvation, and my pessimism about the hardness of earthly life gave way to joyous, positive knowledge of my purpose here.

In spite of my dedication to the Catholic Church, I knew I had been headed in the wrong direction, on an unstable course. I borrowed a thick book on the history of Catholicism to study side by side with the Doctrine and Covenants. I discovered that the line of authority in the Catholic Church was not unbroken since St. Peter, as I had been taught. With all the anti-Popes and the political decisions in spiritual affairs, I realized that the doctrine of Jesus Christ had been corrupted until it was an outward form full of self-contradiction and lacking the spiritual power of the original church of Jesus Christ. The very title "Pope" is mentioned nowhere in scripture—indeed, Christ tells us to call no man father but our Father in Heaven (Matthew 23:9). And although we were taught that the bishops took the place of the Apostles, I could now see that was not true. Many a night I cried myself to sleep as I slowly realized that my beloved Catholic Church was not what I had thought it to be.

I still couldn't see how I could change—the Catholic Church needed me! But the Elders encouraged me to pray for a testimony, and one night, while reading the scriptures before retiring, I had a burning feeling and a sure knowledge that The Church of Jesus Christ of Latter-day Saints was true. I called the Elders at 11:00 P.M. to tell them I would be baptized.

It took a great deal of courage to take that step. But I remembered teaching my students about the prophets of the Old Testament, and asking them if they could be willing to do what the Lord required of them as the prophets had done. I now asked myself the same question: I knew beyond a shadow of a doubt that the Lord was speaking to me through the Book of Mormon, the Doctrine and Covenants, and my own personal revelation from the Spirit. What response would I make? Would I back out, thus denying the very values I had taught all my life?

I think it was very important to me to attend two baptismal services before my own. All the sweetness and happiness of the Mormon people, my own deep peace—the gospel seemed so easy and beautiful to live. In the convent, religion was so hard, so rigid, so artificial, and I was hurt to think of the unnecessary suffering I had gone through in the name of religion. I was so grateful to have found this beautiful church, this true restored gospel.

So on the evening of June 27, 1975, I was baptized at the Westchester chapel by Elder R. Shaffer and confirmed by Leslie Svoboda, my dearest friend and now my husband. I have never regretted the decision I made to be baptized a member of this church. Les and I were sealed in marriage for eternity in the Washington, D.C., temple. My seven years as a member have been the most rewarding of my life—never have I felt so loved; and now, as ward Relief Society president, I can serve and give of myself as completely as I did when I was a nun. I would go through all those years in the convent again just for one day as a married sister in the Savior's church.

I do not say I have had no trials or problems since my baptism—but I like myself much better and feel a deep, underlying peace and joy that is not easily disturbed. I bear my testimony that God lives, that Jesus is truly the Christ, and that the true church of Jesus Christ has been restored to the earth to prepare for Christ's second coming. If prophets were raised up to proclaim his birth in Bethlehem, it is all the more fitting that prophets should be raised up in these latter days to announce to the inhabitants of the earth his second coming as Lord and Judge.

I urge you who read my words to study and pray to know for yourself if the Church of Jesus Christ is truly restored to earth—and don't be afraid to change when you obtain that testimony, for this is the most important knowledge available this side of heaven. The gospel of Jesus Christ is good, strong, and wholesome. Let us live it to the full!

How Do I Get Into This Outfit?

Will Rogers and J. Golden Kimball had something very much in common. They both knew how to tell a story that warmed the hearts of all who heard it. Carr Krueger, a seventy in Littleton Colorado Stake, fits into that same category, whether standing behind a Baptist pulpit as a preacher or now as a sales trainer in his own business. You'll catch his "good ol' boy" flavor as he relates how he got into this Mormon "outfit."

*A*lthough I used to be a full-time Baptist preacher, I never considered myself a minister. To me, a preacher preaches the gospel, but ministers carry quilting frames for the Ladies' Auxiliary. I loved preaching, and I think even as a Baptist I helped bring some people to the Lord. I didn't have all the answers, but then you don't have to be an electrical engineer to throw a switch and get light. The Lord can use anyone who is ready to be used.

I loved my little church in Spice Valley, Indiana. We had standing-room-only evening services. I would say, "Pick out a couple of hymns you enjoy and we'll get to you." After about forty-five minutes of singing their favorites, they didn't need much of a preacher to feel the Spirit there. And the kids enjoyed it: half the congregation was high-school age. They loved it because I wasn't shoving it down their throats, but preached on the "do's" instead of the "don'ts." Those youngsters would fill the trunk of my car with eggs and chickens (not live ones), corn and produce. That's all they had, but the gift meant a lot because they had raised it themselves.

I never was one of those fire-eaters, running around flipping pages, quoting scripture, and trying to convert a bunch of people —I figured I still had a lot of work to do on myself. To me, conversion is like buying land: a new piece of property has to be cleared and built up. You don't stand on a weedy lot and throw rocks at neighbors who are already mowing their lawns. So I never came across as a wild-eyed radical, and always tried to use language people could understand.

I once asked one of the adult deacons in our congregation if he knew anyone in the neighborhood who wasn't a Christian. He took me up to a cabin about a mile from where the paved road ended and we met an older man. As we chatted we could feel a good spirit. I asked him if he had a Bible.

"No, my missus had one, but we buried it with her," he answered.

I asked, "If I gave you one would you read it?" He said his eyesight wasn't too good, but he'd sure love to have one. So I gave him my brown leather-covered Bible that I carried everywhere in those days.

"Have you ever accepted Christ as your personal Savior?"

"No," he replied, "can't say that I have."

"We're all going to shed this mortal body someday. Wouldn't you like to feel he's there to help you over the ditch so you don't fall in?"

He said, "I reckon that would be helpful."

I was using language he could understand, not a lot of flowery words. He would have been scared of a churchhouse full of folks dressed in nice sweet-smelling clothes (he had only a pair of old overalls), but he wasn't afraid of me even though I had on my white shirt.

When I asked him to offer a prayer, he said, "I don't reckon I know how, preacher."

I said: "Have you ever got back with an old friend you haven't seen for years? Would you have any trouble talking to him? Well, that's just the way you should pray—he's the best friend you'll ever have, and he's been waiting a long time to hear from you." On his knees he began to pray: "I don't know you, God. I never saw you, but this young feller says you're my friend. I'd like to give you whatever I've got—me included."

Well, that old man was pretty close to the Lord then—he reached up and put his hand in the Savior's hand, asking for help. Later, the deacon told me he'd been saving him to bring to a revival, but the old man was dead before our next revival, two weeks later.

Well, as I say, even a Baptist preacher can bring someone to the Lord. But the frustrating thing about my work was that I didn't have the answers. I've stood at many an open grave, like the one with a little mother and little bitty kids in Oklahoma, and when the clods hit the coffin lid, it's pretty spooky. The mother said: "Why, Preacher, why? Does the Lord need him more than these kids do?"

I can hear some of those ministers yet. They would pat her on the head and say: "Have faith. The Lord knows what he's doing." Then they'd run like mad, because they didn't have the answers. This is what appealed to me about the Mormons—they take up where everyone else leaves off.

I guess it was my need for religious answers that drew me into preaching. I hadn't intended to be a preacher as a boy—in fact, preachers scared me. I remember when I was growing up in Fort Collins, Colorado—our preacher at the First Baptist Church would beat on the pulpit so hard he would tear the bark off it. But I began to realize the need for religion when I went overseas in the War. I saw many of my friends killed and many foxhole conversions. Often, promises made under those circumstances were quickly forgotten, so I was scared to make those commitments. I didn't drink, I had good morals, but there was still a vacuum in me.

I went out once behind a barracks in Munich, Germany, and had a spiritual experience, committing myself to the Lord. I didn't keep all my promises and I was something of a backslider, but I tried really hard to live better after that experience. When I came back to the States I wanted to go on some kind of a mission for the Lord, and to do that in the Baptist Church you have to go down to the "preacher factory" in Louisville, Kentucky, to be trained.

Soon after my arrival at the seminary, I made a mistake. Some years before, I had married my high school sweetheart. There were problems between us while I was in Europe, and upon my return a court annulled the marriage. My mistake was telling another missionary at the school about the annulment. He assured me his lips were sealed and that I could trust him to tell no one. But I had hardly hit the front door of the seminary before he had told the director all about it, and the director called me into his office.

He said: "Carr, I know you want to go into the mission field. But the thought of a divorced man being supported by the 'widow's mite'—why, if some of those sweet old ladies found out, it could ruin our whole effort." I could just see my career in the ministry going down the tube. I knew I would never have the endorsement of the Southern Baptist Theological Seminary to do any foreign mission work—or pulpit work other than the congregation I already had at Spice Valley. The local selection committee doesn't ask if you set barns on fire or steal from gas stations, and it doesn't matter if the entire congregation is divorced. But they want their preacher to be as sinless and guiltless as the fresh snow.

I guess after that I was too much of a maverick for the ministry. When the Association missionary asked me where my Blue Book was, I said, "I don't know." (The Blue Book gives the total Baptist creed.) "You need to use it more," he told me.

I said, "I'm going to preach what's in the *black* book—the Bible—and if that's not good enough, forget it, friend."

After leaving the seminary, I remarried and got into a direct-selling organization. Many of the people involved in the organization were LDS, but I didn't think of them as Mormons or any other religion. They were beautiful people—cream of the crop—but they never said a word about their religion. It was important to me to make the first move, I guess, because when people said, "You can trust me, brother," I felt like backing into a corner so they couldn't get behind me.

Anyway, when we went to a convention in Salt Lake City, I said to some of my friends: "The Baptists could learn a lot from the Mormons. I wish the Baptists would just treat their people the way the Mormons do." That was all I had to say. That night several couples met us in our room and the Golden Questions were flying all over. Nobody shoved anything down my throat, but we just talked until about two o'clock in the morning.

On the way home to Colorado, I said to Vera: "You know what is the common thread with these folks? They all love one another." I think this is what helped my conversion most. It wasn't doctrine so much, because I couldn't have told you which end Moroni was sitting on. To me, the key was doctrine applied in people's lives. As I thought about all the top-notch people we knew, I realized that the folks we really respected were all Mormons.

Dick Finlinson, one of my friends in the sales organization, invited us to visit them in Oak City, Utah, a little Mormon farming community south of Spanish Fork. I thought it would be wonderful, but my wife said: "They aren't going to let you go down there and relax. They're going to fill you full of that Mormon stuff."

I said, "Oh, they wouldn't do that." Well, they didn't—for about thirty minutes!

Dick is a school administrator, and his wife, Lavon, is like a little bumblebee. He wanted to go from square one to square two, but Lavon was so excited about her testimony that she kept interrupting all the time to relate some bells-and-whistles things that had happened to her. Finally, Dick threw up his hands and said, "We've got to get the missionaries over here."

We got together with two stake missionaries, who set up their little flannelboard under a big cottonwood tree. Since we were there only for a long weekend, they gave us three lessons at once. Right in the middle of the third lesson, I asked, "How do I get into this outfit?"

The younger of the two missionaries replied, "But I still have four more lessons to go!" I thought to myself, *He sure doesn't know much about selling.* I had just given him the buying sign, and all he wanted to do was to tell me more about his product! That was the time to *close the sale!*

He finally said, "Are you ready to get baptized?"

I said, "Let's get on with it."

"First we have to find some clothes for you. And you have to call your bishop for an interview."

I told him I didn't have a bishop, and he replied, "Oh, yes, you do—you just don't know him yet."

Soon I was on the phone long-distance with Bishop Lee Bullock. Lee's just an old cowboy who doesn't talk in a churchy way—I think that's what makes him so successful. He said to me, "Can you swallow that stuff about Joseph Smith?"

I answered, "It doesn't bother me a bit." I told him I used to be an anti-aircraft gunner in the war, and I knew how to aim. Maybe God is fifty million miles out in space, but I recall how he zeroed in on Saul of Tarsus. There Saul was on the road to Damascus, meaner than a gutshot grizzly and looking for Christians to persecute. If God could take aim on Saul and roll him out into the rocks and sagebrush, why couldn't he adjust his celestial "laser beam" just a bit and zero in on a young man in the woods in New York? It made sense to me that the gospel would be restored through a young person—what better tool than an open mind and a willing heart?

Bishop Bullock said, "I guess you're ready."

Anyway, they found some clothes big enough for me, and I

was baptized. I don't know what the rest of the lessons say. I've never heard them.

The Baptist work I came out of is like a telephone cable with one end in the ground and the other end sticking up with little wires reaching out for something to connect to. There are hundreds of thousands of Baptists asking their thousands of questions, committed but searching. That's the way it was with me — then suddenly I found the corresponding connection. All at once everything connected, and there are no frayed or loose ends. The majority of my questions have been answered. Other Baptists are the same. They are hungry for more truth.

Once I spoke at an evening stake conference in Salt Lake City. (The stake president had had a cancellation, and I guess I was all he could find.) I asked, "Let me see the hands of all those who know Baptists." I turned to the missionaries and told them they should go see the Baptists if they were looking for live ones to teach. They are ready. They believe in the Lord Jesus Christ. They believe in baptism by immersion. They have much of the truth, and it's just a natural step from their beliefs to the truths of The Church of Jesus Christ of Latter-day Saints. But only God can open up some of those hearts, so we need to ask for a lot of help from him. I would love them into the Church. You don't chastise them, but help them out of their "chuckhole" and dust them off. That's what the Savior would do — you don't slap the tar out of someone for falling down.

I'm thankful for the Church. I'm so glad I found it. I appreciate the lives of those people who were good examples to me and my wife. While I miss some aspects of my former ministry, I would never go back. Let's face it — I was doing the best I could with what I knew. If a man has a third-grade level of understanding, you can't criticize him for not being ready to go to the moon. But now I have more knowledge and had better be performing at the highest level I can. May the Lord help me to do that.

Daddy, What Have You Done?

A young United Methodist minister could no longer stand up at the pulpit of his church each Sunday morning and preach doctrines he knew were not true. Yet how could he leave the occupation that he felt he had been called by the Lord to pursue? John Harber and his wife, Joyce, helped each other gather the necessary courage, then John informed his supervisor that he must leave the ministry. Only a few months later he was taught the gospel, and shortly thereafter he was baptized. Now visitors at Temple Square in Salt Lake City can find John testifying of his conversion, which seemed to be his turning point as he left the ministry.

*A*s a boy, I was taught to go to church on Sundays, but I'd just as soon slip out to the nearest hamburger stand instead of Sunday School class. When I faced flunking out of college, I knew I had to grow up quickly.

So I joined the Air Force and went to Japan, where, under the discipline of the service, I began to sense a need for a prayerful life—for some sort of direction. In the evenings, after the swing shift, I'd jog down to a park and lie on my back on a picnic table, just looking up into the sky and wondering. I'd wonder about all those stars and what part I had in that great creation. I began asking God where I fit into it all and who I really was. Those prayerful nights helped me develop a strong self-concept and the knowledge that I was a child of God.

When I left the service for college, I found I had outgrown the "dorm scene," with the shaving cream fights and horsing around all night. I felt the need to get on with my life, to get married. I soon found the girl. I had been praying to meet someone like Joyce, and, unknown to me, she had been praying too. Joyce was a student preparing for a nursing mission in South America for her church. I knew she was something special, but after I met her the first time I forgot her last name! Fortunately, I knew what dorm she lived in. When I called the dorm mother, I found there was only one Joyce in the house.

December of 1970 was decisive in my life—I made two important choices: to marry Joyce and to enter the ministry. I had never thought of becoming a minister, yet while attending a Christmas missionary service in the Lakeside United Methodist Church, I responded to an altar call. It was a powerful experience which urged me to become a minister. After our marriage we moved to Illinois, where I enrolled in a three-year seminary.

Ironically, my untested faith was sorely tried by my seminary professor. Here was a man, paid to prepare me for the ministry, telling me that Adam and Eve weren't real, that Jesus may not have been divine, and that the virgin birth might be a myth. Furthermore, I was uncomfortable with the doctrine of original sin. I remember when my oldest daughter was born—I looked through the glass into the newborn nursery at the hospital and whispered to her, "You do not know what sin is." If they had lined up all the Methodist bishops in the world that day, they couldn't have convinced me that the doctrine of original sin was true. I knew it then and I know it now.

Other questions arose as I read the Bible. In Ephesians 4:5 I read about one Lord, one faith, and one baptism. To me, that meant there must be one individual true church—and I was more and more convinced that it wasn't the United Methodist Church. In seminary we learned that all denominations were parts of one big Christian church, and that the differences could be negotiated away. This happened when the United Brethren Church joined with the Methodists: whereas one group previously had preached baptism by immersion and the other by sprinkling, now it is at the option of the individual.

Although these things bothered me, one of the men in my congregation raised a question that really nagged at me. He asked me why I had to get a master's degree to preach the word of God from the pulpit. It was a sincere question that deserved an answer —but I couldn't find a single scripture to satisfy him. And I wasn't satisfied either. I felt empty inside just as I was graduating and preparing to take on my first assignment.

What was I to do? I felt dedicated to the Lord, but I also felt I was living a lie, getting up and preaching doctrines I couldn't believe in. I thought about switching to some other denomination—the Episcopalians, perhaps—but I didn't believe that was the true church either.

I accepted an assignment with a church in Virginia, hoping I would have time to pray and meditate and work out my problems. But new challenges were awaiting me. On my first Sunday with my new congregation, we invited a black couple to services (their Baptist church across the street had burned down recently). As I sat there, one of the most important men in the community and a stalwart member of the congregation entered and saw that couple. "I don't go to church with _____!" he shouted, and he stormed out. Right after the service I went to his home and told him that as long as I was minister of that church, it would be open to everyone. The gospel was quite clear on that point, I informed him, as well as the doctrine of the United Methodist Church.

That was only the beginning of my troubles. I soon learned that being in the ministry is like living in a fishbowl. I remember one morning picking up some beer cans tossed in my yard by a passerby in the middle of the night. I put them in my trash, but the next day the rumor was going around that I was holding beer parties in the parsonage. Our names were dragged through the mudhole.

I worked hard but didn't seem to be able to cover all my expenses. I'd do fifty things every day and still not feel I had done all I could—the people wanted me to be Superman, a "resident God"—and soon I was absolutely drained and in debt. I couldn't even afford shoes for my two daughters. When I was asked to marry a couple, I found myself hoping they would pay fifty dollars instead of the usual twenty-five, just so I could buy the shoes we needed. This sort of thing haunted me: I was trying to be as spiritual as possible, but my family's livelihood was at stake—our home, my life, even my very words. When you preach for a salary, everything you say is controlled.

After my first year, I was required to take an examination qualifying me to be ordained an elder. All graduates had to write a sermon and answer some questions before the senior ministers. I knew I would be asked whether I upheld the doctrine of the United Methodist Church, and as I reviewed that question in my mind I just couldn't see myself answering yes. Before I left, Joyce and I prayed about the problem and then drew a line down the middle of a piece of paper. On the left, I wrote down my reasons for leaving the ministry, and on the right my reasons for staying. The left-hand column filled up so fast I almost had to turn over the page to list all the reasons. Besides my personal reasons for leaving, I just couldn't sustain the church doctrine: I didn't believe in the doctrines of original sin or the Trinity, couldn't accept the notion of a paid ministry—and I rejected the idea that the United Methodist Church was the "one faith" taught in the scriptures.

Joyce and I felt we had our answer. I had to tell my district superintendent I was leaving, so I called for an appointment. I lost courage en route and telephoned my wife for assurance that we were doing the right thing. Joyce has always given me the support I need.

My district superintendent shrugged off my reasons and told me I should stay, not because the Methodist Church was true, not because the Lord and the people needed me—his reasoning was purely economic. Things were tough on the outside, he said. I wouldn't be able to find a job and I had a wife and two daughters dependent on me. But I had decided I would shovel ditches, if necessary, to be a free man again. I promised to finish out the year; but when my congregation heard about it most of them treated me like a Judas. They wanted me out. That hurt most of all, because one of the reasons I was leaving was that I could no longer stand before these people and preach to them things I knew were untrue.

For months thereafter I sent out resumes in response to every possible ad in the paper, but the answers always read "over-qualified" or "underqualified." Finally, after hearing all these no's, I applied for a job as manager of a crisis hotline. I felt sure I could handle that.

But on the day of my interview, my wife, who had been working as a nurse to support us, was in the hospital herself with a bleeding ulcer. We had no insurance, my interview was waiting, and I had no place to leave my two daughters. At last our neighbors across the street came to the rescue. The Sessions were a Mormon family who had quietly been fellowshipping us for about a year, and Geni Sessions now offered to take the kids for me. They had never borne testimony to us, but they had always been there willing and happy to help in any way they could.

When I returned home that night from the interview, I was a broken man. They had said no. I went home to the girls and offered to pay Geni for babysitting, with money I didn't have. She refused it and said she just wanted to help. I could see the pure love of Christ in her face—not a word about her church; just prayers for me and our family, although we didn't know it at the time.

That night I fed my little girls a meal of beans, crackers, and powdered milk—and precious little of that. Their eyes seemed to be asking me: "What have you done, Daddy? We had security when you were a minister, but not anymore. You've blown it!" After putting the girls to bed, I went downstairs to think and pray. I had studied for three years and preached over the pulpit for more than two years, and now it appeared I should have stayed. I was determined to find out that very night if I had made the right choice. I got down on my knees and spilled everything out to the Lord.

I yelled. I wept. It just poured out of me for more than two hours, and when I tried to get up I couldn't. Then, as God is my witness, I felt someone lift me up—I could actually feel someone supporting me, but when I looked over my shoulder there was no one. It reminds me now of the hymn "How Firm a Foundation": "I'll strengthen thee, help thee, and cause thee to stand, upheld by my righteous, omnipotent hand." That is exactly how I felt—in the palm of his hand—and for the first time in months I slept like an infant. I had been liberated from anxiety and knew that everything would be all right. The next morning I could hardly wait to see the sun, to find out what good thing would happen to me. I now understand the words of the Lord: "Come unto me, all ye that labor and are heavy laden, and I will give you rest" (Matthew 11:28).

Shortly after this I had a job delivering mail; and after eight interviews I was at last hired in a sales position for Xerox. Both thrilled and scared, I prayed to find someone in the company who could help me learn the ropes, someone I could trust.

Two days later in a training class at Xerox, a new sales trainer took the floor: "I'm Mike Kuehn," he said. "I'm a very religious person, and I'm here to teach you about an offset press." I felt warm all over and knew he was the one I had prayed to find. After class I took him aside and asked him why he had said he was religious. "Because I didn't want to hear anyone take the name of the Lord in vain in my presence," he said. "I didn't want to hear any filthy jokes either." When he told me he was a Latter-day Saint, I remembered the fine friends we had in the Sessions.

He invited us to his home the next Saturday. No sooner were Joyce and I settled than Mike looked me in the eye and said, "I know The Church of Jesus Christ of Latter-day Saints is the only true church upon the face of the earth." When he bore his testimony to me, I felt consumed. I wanted to say something, but nothing would come out of my mouth. Next he handed me a copy of the Articles of Faith. And there it was, the second article of faith: "We believe that men will be punished for their own sins, and not for Adam's transgression." Here was a church that didn't believe in original sin!

I remember how excited I was as Joyce and I drove home. The next day she couldn't find the address of the Church in the yellow pages—she was looking under *Mormon.* She couldn't believe it when I told her the full, long name of the Church. Unknown to me, she began telephoning. She talked to a stake high councilor for forty-five minutes one day, and he offered to send the missionaries to tell her more.

Joyce was so excited about her conversation with the high councilor that she met me at the front door with the news the missionaries would be coming. *I* wasn't so excited, and I remember being upset with her. But I felt better about it when she left at my dinner plate a short note explaining how important it was to her to find the truth.

On Saturday night a president of the local seventies quorum and his companion came to teach us. They challenged us to attend church the next day, and we did. My wife was really ready for the message; however, I had a little trouble accepting the idea that I didn't have the authority to baptize my daughter and therefore her baptism was invalid.

When I came to understand that point, I decided to join the Church. On October 9, 1976, Mike Kuehn baptized me, and Joyce was baptized by Mike Sessions.

Things haven't always been easy for us since our baptism, although we are progressing vocationally and financially. We moved to Utah in 1978 and settled in the American Fork

Sixteenth Ward, where I am a stake missionary, ward mission leader, and Gospel Essentials teacher. I also serve as a tour guide on Temple Square. Joyce is a leadership trainer in Relief Society.

We have two beautiful daughters: Heather, nine, and Angela, seven. Our youngest daughter, Jerrina, has graduated to our Father in Heaven and awaits us on the other side. We now have a son Javin Shambu, who came to us from India and is now a part of our eternal family. We love the Lord and love to be in his service.

I Didn't Want to Change

The first time John Reiher walked into the Dover Ward chapel he was a bit conspicuous. He was six-and-a-half feet tall, wearing a black suit, a high Roman collar, and a large silver cross, and he answered to the title "Brother." Today, he's still tall, but he has exchanged his Catholic collar for a business suit, and the members there call him a high councilor.

When the front doorbell rang, I knew it was the two Mormon Elders, so I immediately headed for the back door. As I was slipping out, one of the Elders was there to meet me with his ever-present grin and handshake. "Hello, Mr. Reiher, we were just coming by to visit you," he said pleasantly. I knew I'd been caught again.

There seemed to be no escaping these two; however, in a way, I really didn't want to escape. I had an idea that what they were telling me was true—but I had the rest of my life planned, and it didn't include the Mormon Church. I was a Catholic monk and I didn't want to change.

Nevertheless, my mind and my life *did* change. My transformation from monk to Latter-day Saint consumed years of study, prayer, reflection—and overcoming feelings of uncertainty and insecurity.

When I graduated from high school after twelve years of Catholic schooling, I felt secure in my faith but not in my future. At six foot six I juggled with the prospects of playing basketball on scholarship, or of learning the family business. In time, however, teachers and friends attracted me to a third choice—the full-time ministry of the Catholic Church. I then had the option of becoming a parish priest or entering a "religious community" as a monk. At last I determined to join the Congregation of the Holy Cross, a religious order which, among other things, operates Notre Dame University.

A monk's training involves an arduous seven-year course in theology, philosophy, and other academic subjects. More important, a monk must be willing to abide by three basic vows. First, he must take a vow of poverty, which means he owns nothing in his own name—he is given everything he needs to live, including housing, shelter, car, and clothing. Second, he vows chastity. That means he will not take a wife nor have a family, nor otherwise have sexual relations. Finally, he takes a vow of obedience to whatever his superiors tell him to do. This is the hardest of all, because he must give up his own free will to make decisions about things in his life. (A fourth vow, the foreign missions vow, requires the monk to labor in a foreign country for the rest of his life.)

Several years of formal training at Glostenbury Monastery in Massachusetts, and then in Valatia, New York, and Rolling Prairie, Indiana, were required before I took my first vows. These vows are binding for one to three years, after which the monk may renew his vows for a similar length of time. After that he must take the vows for life or leave the community.

It was decided by my community that I should pursue courses in science, math, and school administration at Austin, Texas. In 1961 I was sent to Wilmington, Delaware, to establish a new monastery and a school. The Bishop of Wilmington met with us to discuss the project: "We would like to see it done in three years, but I have no money to give you." Nevertheless, through much effort, the school was housed in a $1.5-million building within three years—and it was mostly paid for.

Content with this achievement I settled back, very comfortable, secure that no transfer was likely for at least five more years.

On a Sunday afternoon in the fall of that comfortable year, I got a call from my superior: "Guess what...are your bags packed?" He told me I was to be transferred to Uganda, East Africa, and explained to me what I had to do to get ready to leave. "Are you willing to accept your assignment?" I said yes. "Any questions?" "Yes, I have one question. I'd like to know why the change at this time?" He replied, "Well, the brother you are replacing in this assignment just had a nervous breakdown and we're bringing him home." Afterwards I thought I shouldn't have asked the question. But I began my preparations to leave for Uganda.

Despite my apprehensions, the change was wonderful. A beautiful tropical country in equatorial Africa, Uganda became very comfortable for me. I was stationed at Fort Portal, in the cooler, mountainous part of the country, where we had 60 missionaries, 12 parishes, a trade school, a college, a hospital, and about 215 primary schools to run.

The Ugandans fascinated me. The majority of the villagers scattered through the mountains had never heard of Christ. In many of the villages, I was the first white man they had ever met. We tried to help the people through our ministry, and baptized, usually by immersion, about two thousand a month. I found myself very content in that part of the world.

As I said, a Catholic foreign mission is a lifelong assignment, so I had no expectation of ever returning to the United States, except for an occasional visit. But one day I was assigned to drive to the capital, a distance of two hundred miles, to get supplies. While returning over a road that was mostly mud and dirt, I had an auto accident and seriously injured my back and my eye. Soon I was shipped back to the United States, on leave, for further treatment. When the Bishop of Wilmington heard about this, he asked to have me permanently reassigned to Wilmington.

Soon after my return, I applied for a five-year leave of absence from my duties in the ministry to attend the University of Maryland on a DuPont Fellowship, and later to work for the Delaware State Board of Education in curriculum development. I was happy with my work, with nothing to disturb my quiet life. Then one Sunday afternoon I was invited to have dinner with friends of mine, newlyweds, former students. While we were relaxing in the living room, the doorbell rang and two of their neighbors, a Mr. and Mrs. Irey, came in and brought with them a plate of Christmas cakes and cookies along with a copy of the Book of Mormon. They shared them with my friends and then left.

We knew what to do with the cakes and cookies, but the question was, What do we do with the Book of Mormon? When faced with the publications of other religions, we Catholics were always instructed to throw them away. But my friends were curious to hear my opinion, so I finally said, "Well, I think I can read it—it wouldn't bother me." I took the Book of Mormon home and read it during the holidays. This was in 1973.

As I read the Book of Mormon for the first time, I was intrigued by its correlation with the Old and the New Testaments; but I was further puzzled by the apparent change of names, places, and individuals. I didn't really understand what the Book of Mormon was, nor where it came from, but when I finished the book I committed myself to find out more about the Mormon Church.

It wasn't until the following July that the opportunity came along to follow through on that decision. Once again, it was a freak occurrence—an air-conditioning breakdown at my office in 98-degree heat—that drove me home during the middle of the day to do some paperwork.

Soon the doorbell rang and I was confronted with two Mormon missionaries out tracting. I told them that I would like to know more about the Church because I had read the Book of Mormon only recently. Well, if you know anything about LDS missionaries, you know that when they heard that, they immediately came up with a baptismal date in their minds for me.

For about seven months Elder Randall James and his companions (who changed about every two weeks—another thing I didn't understand) visited and taught me. They had no idea I was a Catholic monk, since I was just finishing up my leave of absence, so they kept challenging me to come out to their church. I just kept refusing. They challenged me to pray about what they were teaching me, but I told them I would never pray about it.

After the first discussion, I had an inkling of the truthfulness of what these young men were telling me. But I kept telling them no, that I couldn't accept that there had ever been an Apostasy. I used every excuse I could think of to keep from praying about their message—but the real reason was that I knew that as long as I didn't pray I wouldn't have to make a decision. This was the fifth year of my leave of absence, and I had been looking forward to rejoining the active ministry because I knew I would be taken care of for the rest of my life. I wouldn't have to worry about the electric bill, or the car payment, or the gas bill—and I wasn't about to upset the apple cart of my life by praying about the Elders' message. I was afraid of the answer I might receive.

But they were very persistent young men. They kept coming. If I refused to answer the bell, or tried to slip out the back way, they would split up and catch me. We had a good relationship, but I was not going to make any commitments.

Finally the Elders were about to close down their efforts in my area, so they challenged me for the last time. When they left me that evening, Elder James said to me, "Well, one of these days you'll be baptized." And I thought: *How arrogant of this young man! He'll find out that this will never happen.*

When I returned to my duties in the diocese as Director of Religious Education I was also given the assignment as one of the ecumenical officers—I was to represent the Catholic bishop to all the other denominational leaders in the community. In this capacity I met my first Mormon bishop.

As I sat on committees with other church leaders in an attempt to influence the Delaware legislature on some moral issues facing the community, Bishop Joel Temple and I seemed to be alone on one side, with all the others on the opposing side. Bishop Temple represented the Wilmington Delaware Stake Presidency, and he and I saw eye to eye to such an extent that he invited me to come to his Dover Ward office to discuss some of the issues further.

I went to the Dover Ward on a Wednesday afternoon, but only after making sure I put on my good black suit, high Roman collar, and big silver cross, so that when I arrived he would know I wasn't interested in his church. We talked for several hours, though I insisted that I had been taught by the missionaries and, therefore, knew all there was to know. But I kept coming back to talk to him, to read his materials, and we soon became close personal friends.

One day I was conferring with fifty-four of my parish representatives when my secretary came into the meeting with the message that a Bishop Temple was on the phone, but she didn't know what he was bishop of. (I often kidded him later about how he got through my secretary by using his title.) He invited me to attend a fireside.

Now, I had no idea what a fireside was. I didn't remember seeing a fireplace at the Dover Ward, but I imagined a meeting with hot chocolate and marshmallows. That night I listened to Louis K. Payne, the mission president, and Sister Payne. She spoke on the meaning of the gospel in her life and the life of her family, while President Payne clearly defined exactly what the priesthood really is, how it was lost, and then, finally, how it was restored. I had never really understood what the priesthood really is, though I thought I had participated in it for twenty-three years of my own active ministry. I soon realized I had not.

As I drove home with Bishop Temple, I shared my concerns with him. As usual, Bishop Temple said, "I have one more book I'd like you to read." This book, *The Way to Immortality and Eternal Life,* by President J. Reuben Clark, struck me with its straightforwardness.

This compilation of President Clark's radio broadcasts from the mid-1950s clearly defined for me all aspects of the Apostasy and the Restoration. But it was his references that impressed me. I was familiar with the historical documents he referred to, as we used them in our own church. I spent that whole night checking his references and trying to find flaws and loopholes, but found none.

Here I was confronted with President Clark's writings—I couldn't deny them intellectually, and so I decided it was time to pray. I called the office, canceled my schedule for the next three days, and headed for the Delaware beaches.

Now, the Delaware beaches in mid-February are not prime vacation spots but a great place to escape from everyday things. I went to a retreat house down there and took three days to pray and discuss things with my Heavenly Father—the things Bishop Temple had talked about, the things I had read and the missionaries had taught me. I really wanted to find out whether all of this could possibly be true. Soon it was Sunday afternoon and I had all my answers—but none of the answers I had expected. Not one.

It meant I had to decide whether to make a change or not. That weekend I got all the answers I could possibly ask for as clearly as I could have hoped for from my Heavenly Father.

At first, I even hesitated to tell Bishop Temple about my experiences of the weekend, but I finally asked him, "How does one get baptized into the Church?" Now, in my own mind, I figured I would take six more months at least, but the bishop in his wisdom scheduled the baptism for the following Thursday night. "Let's not rush into it," I said. "It has taken me this long—what's a few more months?" But he replied, "No, John, if you're ready, we want to baptize you as soon as possible." There was only one step left—to be interviewed by the Ward mission leader.

I was interviewed on Monday afternoon by the Dover Ward mission leader. Although he didn't remember me, I remembered him. He was the same man who, years earlier, had called on my friends with the cookies and the Book of Mormon I had later read during the Christmas holidays.

On Thursday, February 23, 1978, I was baptized, and then I began to grow personally in ways that have been more dramatic and meaningful to me than anything else I had experienced in my previous twenty-three years of active ministry.

When I joined the Church, I called my Catholic bishop, but he was unavailable for a week, so I typed a letter of explanation to him. I no sooner left it with the bishop's secretary than the phone in my office rang and the bishop was suddenly able to see me.

I tried to share with him my reasons for joining the Church, but he really didn't want to discuss the matter theologically. He wondered if I had been working too hard, that perhaps I was having a breakdown, or that I had been led astray by some Mormon woman. I assured him that none of those things had happened. It's hard to describe the reaction of my former leaders and professional associates. I recall one Episcopal minister who commented to me, "If I had known you were shopping, I would have been soliciting." I told him that I hadn't been shopping. He didn't understand that.

Since my baptism I've visited the West and had many wonderful experiences in Salt Lake City, including serving as an usher in the Tabernacle on Temple Square. While there I called Elder Randall James, who had taught me for seven months and predicted that someday I would be baptized. Needless to say, he was thrilled that I was now in the Church.

I'm currently serving as one of two single members of the Wilmington Stake high council. (Although I was engaged at one point, I haven't yet found my future wife.) My responsibilities include supervision of missionary work.

I like to tell my conversion story—not that it's different from anyone else's, though my background may be unusual for a Mormon convert. We all, in developing our testimonies, find those answers that are important to us, if we take the time to pray about them and listen to the answers.

I Was Just
Simply Curious

*One scripture does not a convert make, but on one
particular morning eight years ago, reading 1 Corinthians
13:8-12 was the turning point for Church of Christ minister
Norman Carlisle. After reading that scripture, he made a
phone call that resulted in his leaving the ministry. During
the week now, you'll find him working in a shoe store in
Amarillo, Texas. On Sundays, he is serving as Sunday
School president in Amarillo Second Ward, Amarillo Stake.*

When someone says to me, "Curiosity killed the cat," I
quickly add, "but satisfaction brought him back." That is certainly true with me. It was just plain curiosity that prompted me
to call the Mormon missionaries the first time, but satisfaction
made me invite them back again and again. Without that curiosity, I would still be a minister in the Church of Christ.

I first heard about the Mormons in high school. I was studying the Westward Movement, and learned a good deal about
Mormon history. In college I took architectural drawing from a
BYU graduate who was teaching some of the other students
about Mormonism on the side, but I really had no interest at that
time.

Strangely enough, though, whenever in my life I have heard
belittling remarks about Mormons, I have found myself taking it

personally. I couldn't figure out why, but I remember defending the Mormon people on several occasions before I really knew anything about the Church.

After trying my hand as a draftsman, I entered seminary courses at the Amarillo Bible Training Work, a school for future ministers of the Church of Christ. A classmate of mine showed me a copy of the Book of Mormon, which he was planning to throw away. I gave him fifty cents for it and flipped through it, remarking on the pictures—but I didn't read it at the time. My curiosity was aroused, however, and I soon began reading anti-Mormon pamphlets.

I forgot about Mormonism until one of my teachers assigned me to write a paper about the "baptism for the dead" passage in 1 Corinthians 15:29. While I was working on the project, a friend of mine mentioned that Mormons practice baptism for the dead, so I decided to call the missionaries I had seen on the streets of Amarillo.

I had been curious about them for a long time, and now I had a reason to contact them. I called them several times a day for about two weeks but never found them at home. At length I gave up—my paper concluded that baptism for the dead was a false doctrine. But now I wonder how my life might have changed had I reached the Elders at that time.

My curiosity continued to nag at me, and several times I sat down to try reading the Book of Mormon all the way through. But none of the names made any sense to me, the story line was hard for me to follow, and after about twenty pages I felt it wasn't worth the effort.

Upon my graduation from the seminary I plunged into my assignment as minister to the Church of Christ in Eastland, Texas, about 350 miles from Amarillo. After several months the elders of the home church decided I had proved myself, so they announced that I should be ordained to the ministry. They pulled a certificate from the drawer, then each elder signed his name and shook my hand. Later there was a formal service in which I was given the certificate. That was it—I was ordained! I decided that the "laying on of hands" must refer to shaking hands.

I really enjoyed being a minister at Eastland, a growing community of about three thousand. I'm sure I knew half the people in town, and I loved making my afternoon visits to the congregation members. Before I met the Mormon missionaries I really wasn't looking for anything else, and I felt perfectly happy and content in the Church of Christ.

It is important to understand a little about the theology of the Church of Christ. It teaches that it is the New Testament church for the twentieth century, carrying on a tradition of Christian worship which dates from the day of Pentecost. The Bible is the seed from which the church grows. The actual organization began with Alexander Campbell, who brought many reform ideas from Scotland to America. He believed that the church should be patterned after the New Testament model; but curiously he also held that there is no need for Apostles in the church, since the function of Apostles was to write the Gospels.

Today, the Church of Christ is splintered and very diverse: one group opposes instrumental music; another rejects the notion of a paid clergy; "One-Cuppers" take communion from a common cup, while "Mini-Cuppers" use individual containers. There is little cordiality or fellowship among the splintered congregations.

Mainline doctrine is unanimous on few points—but one of them is that women should not take part in services. The ministers of the church teach their own understanding of the scriptures, and I learned a great deal about the Bible by preparing my sermons from scratch, out of a concordance. Sometimes my sermons even departed from Church of Christ doctrine, but they were Bible doctrine—and, as I found out later, close to Mormon doctrine as well!

I was to find out just how close when a couple of Mormon missionaries came to Eastland in September 1975. In this small community they seemed to be everywhere: on the streets, knocking on doors, riding their bicycles.

They hadn't bothered me in a city like Amarillo, but here I was the minister and I had to do something about it. At the same time, my plain curiosity made me want to talk to them, to find out what they believed and how they would answer some of the arguments in the anti-Mormon literature I had read.

Anyway, I went to the library in Abilene and found a book on Mormonism called *A Marvelous Work and a Wonder*. I read it through and, to my surprise, couldn't find anything wrong with the doctrine. Now I *really* wanted to talk to those missionaries—I just couldn't imagine what they were like.

One morning soon after, I was reading 1 Corinthians 13:8-12, which announces that prophecies will cease. I said to myself, "Look, it says right here that these things are going to cease, so those Mormons can't be right." But as I read on, I encountered a second passage: "We know in part, and we prophesy in part. But when that which is perfect is come, then that which is in part shall be done away." My concordance indicated that prophecy would cease *in the eternities*, and suddenly it hit me. Here and now, it is perfectly possible that God would speak through prophets, yet in the eternal state *we* will see God face to face.

I immediately went to the telephone to call the Mormon missionaries, because I wanted to know more about their claim to a living prophet on the earth. I couldn't think of anything else for the rest of the day, and although the missionaries didn't answer, I called them every few minutes—even in the middle of my visiting rounds at the hospital. Finally, around 10:00 P.M., I tried once more, and someone answered the phone. I pulled no bones about who I was or why I was calling (I had heard of ministers playing tricks on the missionaries), but introduced myself as a minister of the Church of Christ and invited them to come to my house at nine the next morning.

The next day I felt very nervous and foolish. When I saw them coming up the walk to my house I decided I was going to tell them I had changed my mind about wanting to talk to them.

But when I opened the door a gust of wind hit me, and all of a sudden I felt calm and cool all over. Now I know the Holy Spirit

accompanied the Elders, but at that time I didn't really understand what had happened. After a little small talk, I said: "I hear
you teach lessons. I want you to start off on lesson one and go all
the way through."

Their mouths fell open. One said to the other, "Yeah, and
how long do you think that's going to last?" But they had my
attention from the very first. Although I didn't in the beginning
do any of the reading or praying they asked me to do, I kept
inviting them back. I was surprised to find that they had a sense
of humor, that they had personality. And when they bore their
testimonies, you knew they knew it was true. When members of
my congregation who had encountered the missionaries spoke to
me about it, they would say, "You know, brother, the way they
look and talk, you would think they actually believed it themselves."

After the Elders had given me the second lesson, I sat down
and read perhaps thirty pages of the Book of Mormon and I
sincerely prayed about it. Right then I knew it was true. But I
didn't know what in the world to do about it—or do with it!

It was a small testimony to start with; in fact, if the Elders had
not come back, I probably would not have joined the Church.
But they did come back, and I began to study as never before,
looking up scriptures on every subject they mentioned even in
passing. Things just really started falling into place, and I
remember one Elder asking me several times during one lesson,
"Who is teaching this—you or I?" All the questions I had always
wondered about were becoming clear. For example, a few
months earlier I had given a sermon on the Trinity. My reading
showed me that there had to be three separate personages and
that God had to have a physical body like his Son's; so when the
missionaries taught that concept, I was very receptive.

I finally concluded that no other church taught these truths. I
wrote a letter of resignation to the leaders of my congregation,
explaining that after much study and prayer I knew that Joseph
Smith was a prophet and I could not continue preaching in the

Church of Christ. But I didn't mail the letter until the missionaries gave me the fourth lesson. When they shut their scriptures and looked up at me, I said, "Well, I've got something to show you." I handed them the letter of resignation. They were stunned—and, after the initial shock wore off, thrilled.

Since I had a week's Christmas vacation ahead, I decided I would mail the letter from my parents' home in Amarillo. After a few days, I got a phone call from the leadership asking me what in the world the letter meant. I told them I would talk to them about it on my return, and when I did I stuck to my decision.

I said nothing to my family, but when I returned to Eastland the whole community was popping. It seemed everyone knew about my conversion, even those who weren't members of either church. After I formally resigned my job, I went to my first Mormon services at the little branch nearby. I was shocked.

The first thing I saw was a plump little lady getting up to teach a Sunday School lesson. (In the Church of Christ, women are permitted to sing, but that's about all.) When they passed the sacrament, here were these little cups of water—instead of wine. I nearly slid out of my chair. But after discussing these little differences with the Elders, I had no real problem; it just took a little getting used to.

At last I was baptized in Weatherford, Texas, on December 30, 1975, and then I returned to Amarillo. My family felt I had been brainwashed. I expected that my friends, who knew I had read much anti-Mormon literature, would be falling all over each other to get in the true church once they found out what Mormons really believed. Well, it hasn't happened that way, but whenever I meet members of the Church of Christ I always ask them to compare their church with the model in the scriptures. If they do, they will see that theirs is not the New Testament church.

Believe it or not, I wasn't really worried much about not having a job, even after I finally resigned from the ministry. Of course, I had to find employment right after I got back to

Amarillo, since I had only a car full of gas and five dollars to my name. I arrived on a Saturday night, and by Monday afternoon I was working in a warehouse.

I have now graduated from the LDS Business College in Salt Lake City, where I took courses in marketing and sales. I am working for a large nationwide shoe company. I'm thankful to be a member of the Church. I serve currently as Sunday School president in the Amarillo Second Ward, after having taught Primary and Sunday School and served in an elders quorum presidency.

Many times I have wished I had joined the Church earlier. But I didn't believe in modern prophets such as Joseph Smith until I read that one scripture and prayed about it. I hope that through my story others will see that the Church of Jesus Christ, as established in New Testament times, has been restored and is here for them to accept.

I Knew I Was
Their Target

A mixture of a caring Primary teacher, fifteen miles of mountain roads, and lots of ice cream and cake was the perfect recipe for the conversion of Frank Tupp, a former United Methodist minister, and his wife and family of five children.

*N*early one hundred years after Joseph Smith was released from Liberty Jail, Clay County, Missouri, I was born nearby. But my first contact with Mormons would not come for many years.

Reared as a Baptist, I occasionally attended other churches in my youth, and it was in a small Methodist church that I had my first religious experience. One Sunday evening they showed a movie about a young man from a farm family who had committed himself to spend his life as an agricultural missionary. I was touched by this and felt that God was calling me to dedicate my own life to full-time Christian service. From then on I told everyone that I was planning to become an agricultural missionary as my life's work.

When I grew into my teens our family moved to Colorado for a short while, where I had my first association with Mormons. In high school I came to know two sisters from a Mormon family; they were "different" in a nice sort of way, and I had a lot of respect for them. I will always wonder whether I would have accepted the gospel at that time if they had introduced me to it. However, it was during the following Christmas vacation that a Methodist minister friend of mine persuaded me to begin correspondence study for a license to preach in the Methodist Church.

At first I was reluctant to preach, for I had planned to devote my life to missionary service, teaching people to become better farmers. But after I returned to William Jewell College in Liberty, I got busy preparing to become a minister.

Soon I received approval of the conference board and was appointed minister of the Quinlan, Oklahoma, Methodist Church. That Sunday I gave the first sermon I ever preached in my life, and probably the shortest. I was practically scared to death. What was worse, I had to have another sermon all ready for the next Sunday—and the next.

Finally I was able to prepare a sermon in about two days and take care of other ministerial duties as well. So I decided to continue my college education part-time at Alva, Oklahoma, where I began dating Beverly Olson, who later became my wife. At the end of two more school years I had a wife and a son, Eldon, and we felt strapped to make ends meet. Eventually, when I approached a district superintendent of the Methodist Church in Kansas, he assigned me to work in two adjoining communities, Woodston and Alton. (I was no longer the minister of the Quinlan church.) The combined salaries of the two churches permitted me to continue my school work.

It took me ten years to complete my college degree while also preaching and pastoring at several congregations. Upon graduating I took a vocational aptitude test which indicated that I had little prospect for success in the ministry! According to the test results, I was most fitted to be an architect—but with my growing family and my sense of a calling to the ministry, I didn't see how I could abandon the work I had chosen.

While at Woodston I began to think seriously about the faith to which I had committed myself. I felt I had come to a sincere understanding of the atonement of Jesus Christ and recognized the price paid with his suffering and death for the sins of every human being—including myself. (I didn't come to my present fuller comprehension of the Atonement until I was taught by some Mormon missionaries many years later.) At the same time, however, I was disturbed by a feeling that the organized churches were not really speaking for God, that they didn't really know what God would have them teach and do. I felt that my own teaching was in harmony with the revelations of the Bible, but within the Methodist Church I found no unanimity on any one principle or issue. So I committed myself to pray and meditate on the Bible to strive to learn what God would have me preach.

It must have been about that same time that some LDS missionaries called on my parents. Although they didn't accept the gospel, they accepted from the missionaries a copy of the Book of Mormon, which my father rather facetiously suggested I should read. I looked at the introduction but did not read the book. I knew nothing of Mormons, except that they were sending young men out for two years as missionaries and they believed that Christ appeared to the Indians here on the American continent following his resurrection. I occasionally referred to Mormonism in my sermons—suggesting the merits of a full-time mission for young people in our church as well.

My difficulties with the United Methodist Church continued to grow. When I attended the annual conferences of the church in the mid-1960s I became disenchanted with the church's inviting militant leaders as speakers who used scare tactics to promote their very liberal and humanistic views. The church leaders were doing much experimenting with methods of worship and beliefs; teaching, among other things, the theory that God is dead. In their worship services I felt they were seeking the "form of godliness but denying the power thereof."

In my own congregations I tried to introduce a program called the Undershepherd Plan, which called for the families of the church to be divided into groups of five, with one person appointed as "undershepherd" to keep in close contact with those families and report to the minister on any of their needs. However, the congregational leadership decided they did not want to commit themselves to that kind of effort and responsibility. I tried this in two different communities and no one was interested.

Two additional points disturbed me. One was our never-ending problem with finances. There were very few individuals who tithed or contributed substantially to the church with no strings attached. I was also bothered that most of the work and service in the church was expected to be done by women, old people, and kids. And from my experience, that wasn't far from the way it worked.

As I became more and more discouraged with the ministry, Beverly and I talked about alternatives. We both wished we could have our own home, our own business, or live on a farm and be more independent. As I participated in a ministerial study group on the principles of success and self-motivation, I realized I could not fulfill the goals I really wanted to achieve as long as I remained a minister. At last I made up my mind to leave the ministry. Since then, several people have asked me if I regret the decision—the truth is I have never for a moment wished I were still a minister.

During the summer of 1973 we moved to Portal, Arizona, where my father purchased Cave Creek Ranch, a mountain resort. We began the management of the cottages and apartments, and our children started school in San Simon, about thirty miles away. It wasn't long before the kids started begging us to let them stay after school Tuesdays to attend Primary. Mrs. Norris, their school teacher, offered to drive them home after

Primary, which involved an extra fifteen miles or so for her over the dirt and mountain roads. Since I wanted them to have some kind of church training, I decided that would be better than nothing, so I let them go. This continued for about a year as our friendship with the Norris family grew.

In October 1975 Mrs. Norris invited us over to their house on a Sunday afternoon for ice cream and cake. She said two missionaries would be there, and she thought I might be interested in meeting and visiting with them. I wasn't very anxious to go, but I couldn't think of any way to decline the invitation—the Norrises had been so good to us that I felt almost obligated. Besides, I love ice cream and cake.

On Sunday we arrived at the Norris home. Also present were Elders Hill and Sorensen. I was a little defensive because I knew what their mission was and that I was their target. Elder Hill took the lead, showing a filmstrip, *Man's Search for Happiness,* which taught where we came from, why we are here, and where we go after this life. The idea of the premortal life was not totally new to me, but I had never before heard it taught. As we discussed this and other points, I found myself beginning to argue with Elder Hill. To me he seemed bullheaded, treating his own ideas as facts and mine as theories. I had always found it difficult to discuss religion with people who were not openminded. Obviously, I didn't understand the principle of revelation at that time.

But I stood my ground. As the discussion closed, I inwardly sighed with relief—then, as I relaxed, Elder Hill asked for an appointment to come to our home. "Oh, I don't know," I said, but they didn't back off a bit. Elder Hill asked if Tuesday evening would be all right. "I guess so," I replied. I'm sure they recognized my lack of enthusiasm, but they had an appointment anyway.

Our Tuesday night meetings were not as emotionally charged as the one at the Norris home. When I realized the missionaries were not trying to force anything on us, I began to relax and ask questions. When they offered me the Book of Mormon, I took it with real interest—I wanted to find out what it said about the origin of the Indians on this continent. As I read I looked for ideas I could not agree with. I never found one.

During one discussion, the missionaries challenged us to follow the Word of Wisdom by giving up tea and coffee. Now, I had always had coffee with my breakfast. Was I going to give it up just because they said it was wrong? By giving up coffee, I would be taking that first definite step toward accepting their teachings, and I wasn't ready for that. But Beverly took care of that for me. Next morning there was no coffee for me on the breakfast table. I chuckled to myself, "Boy, they sure got her!" Now, more than seven years later, there is still no cup of coffee for me on the table—or anywhere else.

Soon the missionaries challenged us to be baptized on January 15 and arranged for the ward mission leader to interview us. I cancelled the interviews because I didn't think we were ready to accept the teachings of the Church—with the exception of Beverly, who seemed to be ready. She would have gone ahead but decided to wait for the rest of us. January 15 came and went. Though we didn't accept the challenge for baptism, nevertheless we did begin to attend Sunday School and sacrament meeting, and we have attended regularly ever since.

It was not until the following summer that things began to firm up in my mind. I suppose that deep down I believed in The Church of Jesus Christ of Latter-day Saints, but I had not received that burning testimony of which they spoke. I had first to resolve two major questions in my own mind.

First, did an apostasy in fact take place as prophesied in the Bible? To me, history pretty well proved it. I decided that the Protestant churches could not collectively claim to be Christ's true church because of the great variety of doctrines—some in direct contradiction to each other. Collectively, they are a mass of confusion, and I knew that God is not the author of confusion. Most Protestant churches do not even claim to be Christ's one true church; they were organized by men rebelling against

Roman Catholicism, and none of them could substantiate receiving authority from Christ himself.

This left only two remaining possibilities: the Roman Catholic Church and The Church of Jesus Christ of Latter-day Saints. Both claim to have authority directly from Christ. But if the apostasy predicted in the Bible did take place, then the Roman Catholic Church has lost its chain of authority. History shows that it no longer has the New Testament organization, with Apostles and prophets, nor do its practices harmonize with the scriptures. The Mormon Church remained the only choice for me.

But a second question remained: Could the Mormons be right in their claim to a restoration of Christ's true church for the last dispensation of time? I could see that the LDS principles and teachings were consistent with those of the scriptures, and that the Church was organized according to the New Testament pattern. I was now sure that the other churches were not true, and I suspected that the LDS Church was the right one.

So I called the rest of the family together to see how they felt. I knew that if the LDS Church was true we should become members, and I discussed it with them—particularly with my oldest son, Eldon, whose support I would need if we were going to be baptized as a family. Eldon said, "Yes, that is probably right." So we decided to go ahead.

When we contacted the ward mission leader to make arrangements for the baptisms on the following weekend, we learned that Rae Anna Norris, a daughter in the family who had introduced us to the Church, was to be baptized that Saturday evening on her eighth birthday. I told him we certainly didn't want to detract from this special occasion for her. He assured us our baptisms wouldn't do that. Little did we realize how much more it would mean to that family to see us all baptized together.

On Saturday, September 4, 1976, all seven members of our family were baptized and confirmed. My sons and I received the Aaronic Priesthood, and a short time later I was ordained an elder. Beverly and I went to the Arizona Temple on December 17, 1977, to be sealed with our five children for eternity. Since then our two older sons have received the Melchizedek Priesthood and are serving missions for the Church, one in Japan and one in Hawaii. Our third son is also planning on a mission soon.

My testimony of the truthfulness of the gospel has continued to grow ever since my baptism. I am especially grateful for the emphasis the Church puts on rearing the family in righteousness and preserving it for eternity, through family home evening and through teaching scripturally correct principles. I am grateful for this opportunity to share my experiences and testimony, and hope that this will in some way help others to make their decision for Jesus Christ and his restored church in these last days.

What If . . . ?

There is a time to ponder and a time to pray. It took the humble tears of a new missionary to help Ralph Drake understand that the pondering had gone on long enough. Now it was time to pray. This former Disciples of Christ minister did just that, and now he is teaching others to do the same as a high priest in Kentucky.

*O*ccasionally entire lives are changed by chance meetings between two people—even momentary meetings. So it was when I roomed with Hollis Scott, an unassuming Latter-day Saint, at a business seminar in Washington, D.C., just over five years ago.

How would my life be different today had we not met? What if I had been roomed with someone else—or hadn't gone at all? What if Hollis had not lived his religion? What if he had been hesitant to tell me about his church? Suppose he had not read the scriptures nightly as he had been counseled to do?

This I do know—my life has been changed, and I believe God had a hand in my meeting with Hollis Scott. My experience has given me the resolve to be the best person I can be, in case God puts me in a situation where I can help someone else to accept the restored gospel of Jesus Christ as Hollis helped me.

My story is happy and sad: sad insofar as it took me so long to find this gospel after serving more than ten years as a minister of the Disciples of Christ; happy in that I found it early enough in life to be of service to others.

I was born in Kentucky about forty miles from Louisville, at the old Drake homestead where my granddad was born in 1861. When I was in the eighth grade I told my dad I wanted to be baptized a Christian, but he advised me to wait until I was sure. Finally, in my high school years I took that step and began thinking about the ministry. Soon after being baptized I heard about a school for ministers in Tennessee where I could study whether I had money or not. I enrolled in this Disciples of Christ seminary, and in my third year there I got married.

At Johnson Bible College we tried not to identify ourselves with any of the different factions of the church. We dreamed of the time when the polarizations among Christians would dissolve. I personally could see no reason why whole denominations split up over simple conflicts like belonging to a missionary society or having instrumental music in church. Wherever I served, I tried to be a unifying force.

In seminary I became intensely interested in the analysis of every thought in the Bible, and I learned to study that book in the original Greek. I was always asking embarrassing questions. What did the Apostle Paul mean by baptism for the dead, for example? (1 Corinthians 15:29.) They sidestepped that question, along with others. Why was the church set adrift anciently without apostolic authority to keep us unified in the faith? Another thing that continued to disturb me over the years was the notion that people would be punished for their sins by frying for eternity. I could not believe that a God of love and mercy would do that. A common rejoinder to these questions was: "Where the scriptures are silent, we are silent: where they speak in matters of faith, we also speak."

Despite these problems, I became a fairly successful minister, although my beginnings were humble enough, as I started out hitchhiking weekly to a little church in Hot Springs, North Carolina. Later my career took me to churches in Georgia, Indiana, Illinois, and Tennessee. I also attended seminary at Butler University for a while, and was recognized statewide as Minister of the Year in a three-year accomplishment, where I also served as president of the local ministerial association.

Suddenly my career in the ministry was interrupted. While I was serving in Illinois, my wife and I began having problems and my marriage fell apart. In the years that followed I found that a divorced minister would not be accepted in most congregations, so I left the ministry (at Cleveland, Tennessee).

My non-church jobs included eight years in insurance and real estate, and seven as a high school teacher. Then nine years ago I went to work for the state of Kentucky, where I now work. In this capacity I attended a seminar in Washington, D.C., on archives and records management. My roommate for the two-week course was Hollis Scott, who worked in the archives at Brigham Young University. He was the first Latter-day Saint I ever met. Here was a very unassuming person, humble and easy to get along with—an unusual character and spirit. I noticed that at restaurants he always declined offers of drinks, and that he read from the Bible each evening before bed.

On our second Sunday there, he mentioned that he was going over to the new temple and asked if I had seen it. I didn't know anything about the new temple. I thought he must be Jewish, talking about a temple. But he described it and showed me a picture. I was flabbergasted. What a beautiful thing! I asked if I could go with him, and he said yes, but that I couldn't go inside. That really intrigued me, so I asked him if I wasn't good enough to go inside the temple. After we got past that point, he gave me a book about the history of Mormons.

I didn't read it then; but sometime later when I knew I would meet Hollis again after a similar meeting in Denver, I hurried and read it. It intrigued me—not the history, for I know that can be terribly glossed over, but the faith of the people. I told myself that this story would be impossible without the hand of God in it.

As the Denver trip approached, I called Hollis and asked if my wife and I (we had remarried some years after our divorce) could spend a few days with him in Utah. When we arrived, I was thrilled with the spirit I felt around him and his wife. I was given the VIP treatment at the Visitors Center on Temple Square and at the Beehive House, and we had a fine meal at the Lion House. Wherever I went there I found engaging people and some wonderful ideas.

I was struck by the idea that we had existed before we came into mortality. I had always thought that might be true—how could Christ be our model if we hadn't come from heaven as he did? In my hour or two at the Visitors Center I was amazed that the Mormon Church agreed with me and my views on the Bible, whether it be from the King James Version or the Greek texts I had studied. Before leaving, I was asked if a couple of missionaries could come to our home. I said, "You mean our home in Kentucky?" I thought it was a little out of hand to send someone clear from Salt Lake to Kentucky to tell me more about the Church. When they explained about missionaries in my own town, I signed a card, thinking I hadn't committed myself to anything other than finding out a little more.

After several weeks at home, I said to my wife, "I guess the missionaries aren't coming." I was glad—but also somewhat disappointed. I believe it was two nights later that I heard a knock on the door and looked outside. Two people stood there. They said something, and I said, "No, I'm not interested," not realizing who they were. Then they held up the card: "Didn't you sign this card?"

Well, that was the beginning. We started to investigate, and the Elders later invited my wife and me to church. Surprisingly, as much as we enjoyed the service, we didn't see the missionaries there. When they visited us again, they told us they were sorry we hadn't made it to church. But we had been to church! The next week we went back at a different time, but none of the friendly people we had met the week before were there. This was a whole new bunch of friendly people! Finally we figured out we were going to a different ward than the missionaries attended.

A long time afterwards the missionaries told me that someone had written on my referral card, "Drake wants to know everything." And I guess I did, for we studied together for months and months, back and forth. I wasn't necessarily resisting, but I couldn't make up my mind. I didn't until I met a certain Elder who showed me a film about the background and history of the Book of Mormon lands.

I had read the entire Book of Mormon, but I had never done that one thing that is necessary for true conversion to take place. This new Elder came in without great sophistication and knowledge, but completely consumed with faith and conviction. He told me that all of the study would never do any good until the Spirit of God moved me. "What does the Book of Mormon say?" he asked, tears running down his face. I said, "The Book of Mormon says you ponder these things and then you pray." He asked me if I had been pondering these things, and I replied that was exactly what I had been doing. "Have you prayed?" he asked. I answered, "No."

On their next visit the Elders were showing the film, and scenes of giant wheels and ruins of temples in South America were passing in front of me. I knew a little about that part of the world, and I began to recognize the truth of it all—my objections started to fall apart. As the movie continued, I was sitting there praying. "Well, what do you think?" the missionaries asked.

"About the film or the Church?" I replied.

They wondered if I felt the Church was true, and I answered, "I am ready to be baptized." I looked at my wife and said, "I don't know what she thinks, but I am ready."

Mary and I were baptized on December 17, 1979, and I'm currently serving as secretary in the high priests quorum.

I find there is much common ground between the Disciples of Christ and the Mormon Church. Many Latter-day Saints are familiar with the Disciples of Christ from the fact that Sidney Rigdon, Parley P. Pratt, Lyman Wight, and others left that faith and joined the restored Church in the 1830s in the Kirtland, Ohio, period. But the Mormons are way ahead in their understanding of the scriptures which both churches accept—and I would have known that sooner if I had just asked the Lord. As soon as I asked and prayed for an answer, I knew it was true. At such a time, you know! You just know, because the Lord himself is revealing it.

I have seen in the Church a real love and affinity for one another. Since joining, I have had many spiritual experiences. As home teacher to a family in the midst of losing their father to heart disease, I saw more fully what Christianity is all about. It was demonstrated in the beautiful acceptance of this death by the family and all their friends—something of the Spirit of God I had never seen or shared before, though I had conducted many funerals.

My wife and I are very happy being of service to others in the Church. We would recommend it to all who are seeking their Heavenly Father. And we are most thankful to Hollis Scott for the kind of life he and his wife live.

I Felt
I Was Saved

Ronald Palmer, son of a Baptist minister, was called to the ministry by his congregation in Florida. After just a few short months he realized that if he met the Lord face to face he would be taught one doctrine and one doctrine only. Thus started his quest to find that one doctrine. Brother Palmer, his family, and thirteen relatives have since joined the Church. Brother Palmer is now an air conditioning contractor in Largo, Florida. He is high priests group leader in Seminole Ward, St. Petersburg Stake.

I found the true religion in the last place I expected—the Mormon Church. And I might not have found it at all, in the midst of my investigations into many creeds, had not a bishop's wife refused to give me a Book of Mormon unless I would promise to read it.

As a child, I always felt close to the Lord. My father, a Baptist minister, taught me that I was saved, and this is what I felt. But in my teens and early twenties I drifted away from church and felt uncomfortable there, though I went to please my wife. I just didn't like sitting there listening to a preacher, so I began to pray for help.

I really did want to serve God, because everything else seemed so temporary—the only permanent thing is our relationship with the Lord. As I was praying one day while driving down the freeway, I felt an overwhelming desire to get involved in the church. I joined the Southern Baptist choir, taught Sunday School, and was called to serve in the quorum of deacons that oversees the spiritual affairs of the congregation. When I tried my hand at preaching, the congregation voted to make me the minister. I served for several months and ran an air-conditioning business at the same time.

Shortly after I was called to the ministry, I became curious about the beliefs of other churches. I wanted to know what the truth was. I knew that if Christ stood before me he would not teach conflicting doctrines, and I couldn't understand how Christian ministers could be inspired to do so. I wanted to know why there was so much confusion. Why were we not all of one church, one faith, one baptism? Why didn't God speak to us today?

I began investigating other religions, finding what I considered to be truth as well as error in many of them. I discussed considerably with the Jehovah's Witnesses, the Catholics, the Presbyterians—I began to feel that perhaps the Lord wanted me to collect as much truth as I could and start my own church!

Many churches have sprung up in this way, particularly among the Baptists. But deep down I said to myself that any church I set up would be just another among many churches, and I had better be sure the whole truth couldn't be found in an existing church before I started one of my own. The last place I expected to find it was in the Mormon Church.

I had been taught that Mormons weren't even Christians, but I was so thirsty for knowledge that I tried to track down a copy of the Book of Mormon. Most of the ministers I knew already had one, so I began calling around to find one for my library. When I called the local ward bishop's home, a woman answered and said I could have a used one of hers.

When I went over to pick it up, she told me I could have it on the condition that I would read it. I agreed, and I kept my word. While reading, though, I wasn't satisfied—I wanted to know specifically what the Mormons taught. So I called the woman again and she promised to send over the missionaries.

My wife, Maxine, was really opposed to this. She hadn't objected when I talked to the Presbyterians, but felt that Mormons and Jehovah's Witnesses were just too "far out." Because of Maxine's opposition, I met the missionaries elsewhere — at a Mormon patriarch's home.

I explained to the missionaries that I had no desire to convert, just to learn. I never challenged them as they conducted their lessons, as I simply wanted to find out what they believed. After a certain point, they wanted me to accept a baptismal date, but I told them I didn't feel justified in doing that. Nevertheless, they wrote down a date for me — I didn't even know what it was, although we continued to talk.

But my wife's opposition became a barrier between us, and I decided I'd better stop meeting with the missionaries. Then my wife and I took a trip to my childhood home at Pensacola, Florida. There I visited with the minister who had married us, and I asked him what he thought of the Mormons. "Oh, I know all about the Mormons," he said, and he pulled down the Book of Mormon and the Pearl of Great Price. As I questioned him, he turned to the Book of Moses and read the passages about the plurality of Gods. This was intended to dispel my interest, for he felt that eternal progression was not a Christian doctrine. However, I went back home more determined than ever to learn all I could about Mormon beliefs.

As I reviewed the discussions, I was attracted by the concept that we could have Apostles and prophets sent by the Lord in these latter days. I had often wondered how God could leave us in such a quandary, in the midst of all these denominations, and it seemed logical that he would speak directly to us once again. I had dreamed how wonderful it would be to live during the time of the ancient prophets and Apostles, to hear the doctrine from them. I like to think I would have believed in Christ even then. Therefore, when the missionaries said God had sent new prophets and Apostles, I could not in good conscience deny the possibility. I didn't know whether it had truly happened or not.

So the missionaries challenged me with Moroni 10:4-5. They told me that if I were sincere and asked with real intent, the Lord would manifest the truth of it to me. To show my sincerity and intent, I stopped drinking coffee and tea (I had already quit smoking when I became a minister). Further, when the Mormons observed fast Sunday, I fasted with them.

My wife was alarmed at all this, because it was an indication that I was leaning their way. She told me, "When we pray, I get one answer and you get another." I reminded her that I was studying hard and pondering the scriptures, whereas she wasn't. In addition, I had been praying to know if Mormonism was true, while she had been praying that I would be shown that it was false.

Two weeks passed, and things were getting back to normal, when Maxine suddenly announced that while she had been praying it had come into her mind that her husband was seeking to serve God and that she should follow her husband. The impression was so strong that it had convinced her completely. As I was leaving for a discussion with the missionaries, she said, "Do I have time to get ready? I know nothing about the Mormon Church except that it is true, and I'm ready to be baptized."

I was shocked. Although I had already decided to be baptized, I hadn't told her yet of my feelings. But she had never met a Mormon nor heard a discussion!

I was baptized the next Saturday, which was the date the missionaries had written down to begin with. I now learned that the ward had been fasting and praying for an organist. They had built a brand new chapel with a big beautiful organ, but there was no one to play it. Well, I could play, and the next day I received the Aaronic Priesthood, was ordained a priest, and was called to serve as ward organist. When my wife came to church that day for the first time, she asked where her husband was.

"Don't you hear him?" they answered. "He's up there playing the organ."

Over the next week my two sons took the lessons with my wife, and I baptized the three of them the following Saturday. Soon I was active in teaching Sunday School along with my wife, who also became president of the Young Women. Eventually I was called to be elders quorum president.

Now, my parents were very upset at all this. My father even went around and apologized to all my relatives on my behalf. So I started teaching my father out of the Bible, showing him as the missionaries had shown me that the authority to baptize was not in the Baptist Church. He and my mother agreed to read the Book of Mormon if I would just leave them alone—but as they read, looking for faults, they humbled themselves. They soon had a testimony that the Book of Mormon was scripture, and four months after my baptism they asked me to baptize them.

This was, of course, an additional testimony to me. Soon my father and I were going around teaching about the Restoration to the same relatives he had earlier apologized to for my actions. Within one year from the date of my baptism, my father and I baptized thirteen members of my family, including my grandmother, cousins, nieces, and an aunt and uncle. A cousin and a niece have graduated from BYU, and my cousin later served a mission.

When I joined the LDS Church, the members of my Baptist congregation withdrew from me completely. The minister told them I had gone astray and would return someday. That was over twelve years ago, and I still think joining the Church was the greatest thing that ever happened to all of us. I'm now serving as high priests group leader. My father and mother have recently served a full-time mission in New York.

I enjoy doing missionary work, particularly among the Baptists. When I meet with them, I ask them what Christ really means to them. I ask them who God is, and where they came from before this life. When they point out to me that they are saved by their belief in Christ, I tell them that the Bible says the devils also believe (James 2:19). Are the devils saved, then? They insist that faith alone is necessary to salvation—but James clearly teaches that faith without works is dead (James 2:20). As Mormons, we too believe that we are saved by grace, but only after all we can do (see 2 Nephi 25:23).

Many of these people have an open mind and are willing to listen and understand. As I reflect on my own experience, I can picture the darkness of my former condition. I had one little candle: my understanding that Jesus died for my sins. My candle was the Baptist Church. Now, some people can't take their eyes off that candle to see a greater light growing to the power of a thousand-watt bulb. Although the candlelight is better than total darkness, it isn't as good as the full truth. As a Baptist, I was thirsty for doctrine and not afraid to take my eyes off that candle to look around at what the Lord might be doing in these last days.

Our family is very happy in the Church. We will be ever grateful to that bishop's wife for having the courage to commit me to read the Book of Mormon. Without that commitment, I would probably have left the book to collect dust in my library. Now I love the Book of Mormon, along with the Bible.

For me the gospel is like a rosebud. As a Baptist minister, I thought I understood and appreciated it, but my understanding has blossomed and is now in full bloom. We are busy serving the Lord as we know he would have us do.

We Waited for Six Years

William and Alexandria Schnoebelen, members of the Milwaukee Second Ward, both served in the Catholic clergy, Brother Schnoebelen as a parish priest, Sister Schnoebelen as a nun. They both left the Catholic Church during the backlash of the Second Vatican Council. He is currently elders quorum president, while his wife teaches in Relief Society. Brother Schnoebelen is currently writing a book on contemporary Christian religions, which is designed to help investigators.

*I*t's pretty remarkable when a former Catholic priest marries a former nun, but it's even more remarkable when they end up joining The Church of Jesus Christ of Latter-day Saints together. Both my wife and I had been reared in strict Catholic families, and we both felt the "call" to a religious life at a tender age. Although we did not meet until conflicts and questions had driven us away from Catholicism, our early lives were shaped by the best the Catholic faith had to offer.

As a little girl, my wife used to rise before dawn and spend several hours out in the back yard in rapt meditation. Even so young, she was drawn to a life of prayer and contemplation. And for my part, I knew I wanted to be a priest even before I entered kindergarten. It was the highest calling a young Catholic boy could wish for. I used to take my mother's old bed sheets and, with the help of crayons, convert them into "vestments," with which I would pretend to celebrate the Holy Sacrifice of the Mass (Oreo cookies served for communion wafers).

After high school, my wife was attracted to the Franciscan contemplative life, so she entered the Order of the Poor Clares. My courses directed me into the minor seminary.

The times were tempestuous for those entering the religious life. The year 1967 saw the implementation of many liturgical and ritual changes ordered by the Second Vatican Council—and much theological change was upon us as well. While still in high school, I was profoundly disturbed by a young priest full of ecumenical fervor who taught us that the miracles of the Bible were actually normal, natural happenings.

After centuries of maintaining an icy aloofness above the turbulent seas of liberal scholarship, which attempted to "demythologize" the scriptures and make them "relevant" to our times, the Catholic Church was crumbling right into the waves of ecumenism. No longer were we the one true church. No longer was the Catholic priesthood an almost magical cadre of supreme leaders which no lay person would ever question. Fundamental assumptions of Catholic doctrine were falling by the wayside, and my wife and I were caught in the avalanche.

College brought me serious doubts about my vocation to the priesthood. As a junior, I took a course in Christian ethics from a professor who advocated masturbation, sexual freedom, and Marxist philosophy as the keys to Christian behavior. I considered dropping out over these conflicts, but I was afraid of "losing face," so I stuck it out.

My studies became more and more dismaying, however. It seemed that the crystal clarity of Christian Aristotelianism was being drowned in the muddy waters of Camus, Sartre, and Marcuse—secular philosophies such as phenomenology, existentialism, and Marxism had relegated the time-honored work of Aquinas to dusty library shelves.

My ordination to the priesthood, although ritually impressive, left me feeling somehow empty. After the bishop laid his hands on my head, I felt little difference in myself. It seemed I had been ordained to a priesthood which no longer knew precisely what it was, to lead the people in directions that were no longer clear.

In my active ministry I felt inadequate to help my parishioners with their problems. The older people were wonderful, holding as they did to their simple faith and spirituality. But with the younger generation I felt as though I were walking on a paper-thick carpet of despair. More and more edicts came from the bishops, each more bewildering than the last. We could now eat meat on Friday. We no longer had to fast during Lent and Advent. Things previously regarded as grave sins were brushed away, and the supposedly unchangeable grandeur of the Latin Mass was so utterly trivialized as to render it comical.

The people suffered from too much change too fast. They felt lost, and so did I. "The church is evolving," I would say when they came to me for help. "We are letting the fresh air of ecumenism blow through the church—we must trust the bishops to know what they're doing."

Finally, I had to ask for a leave of absence. My superiors were sympathetic and gave me a job teaching music in a Catholic high school. Even here the "new" church mocked me. The simple solemnity of the Gregorian chant which once accompanied the liturgy was being replaced by rehashed folk music and banal modern tunes on electric guitars and drums. I was forced to direct music that would have been unthinkable in Catholic sanctuaries only a few years earlier.

To keep my sanity, to feel as though I were doing good somewhere, I volunteered to work weekends at a drug rehabilitation center in Dubuque. Here I met my future bride and eternal companion.

Alexandria had left her order for the same reasons for which I had left the priesthood. The bishops were pressuring the contemplative orders to get out in the world and do something more "relevant" than gardening, praying, and making rosaries. Alexandria had left in disgust, and found herself working beside someone who had similar conflicts with the church. We were kindred souls, but the idea of interacting with a woman terrified and excited me at the same time. In spite of it all, we were made for each other.

After a gentle, nine-month courtship, we were married in a civil ceremony on May 31, 1974. We had both soured so much on the Catholic Church that we could not bear a church wedding. I looked for a job in Dubuque, and ended up working as a security guard. My wife started managing a golf club.

Just a few weeks after our wedding, a friend told us about two missionaries who had come to her door. She was excited by their visit, and told us, "They're two guys from the Mormon Church. When they talk about religion, they sound just like you two." We begged her to give us their number, and we called for an appointment immediately.

The Elders were astonished at our eagerness and openness to the gospel. They would bring up very tentatively some doctrine like baptism for the dead or eternal marriage, half expecting us to laugh them out of the apartment. To their amazement, we had no trouble in accepting any of it. We had only one problem—the perceived loss of stature of Mary. Both of us had been devoted to Mary and said rosaries every day; but when we learned the LDS Church taught the existence of a Heavenly Mother as well as a Heavenly Father, we were relieved.

The Dubuque Branch sacrament meetings were held in a Seventh-day Adventist meeting hall. We were at first dismayed at the stark simplicity of the services and all the noisy infants, but we soon felt the spirit of the gathering and were quietly—definitely—impressed.

We were taking two lessons a week, when suddenly I was stricken with typhoid. The sickness and lengthy hospitalization cost me my job as a security guard. The financial situation was getting desperate, so I took a job at a scrap-melting operation in Milwaukee.

The Elders assured us there were missionaries in Milwaukee, and when we arrived we called the number of the Milwaukee Ward bishop listed in the phone book. I identified myself as an ex-Catholic priest interested in joining the Church, whereupon the person at the other end hung up on me!

This threw us into a dilemma. We thought that perhaps we had gone about this in a wrong way. Previously, we had dealt with a "measly" branch president, and we thought that Mormon bishops might be like Catholic bishops—you don't just call them up unless you're a high-muck-a-muck yourself. So we waited for missionaries to come to us.

We waited six years! In the meantime, we looked into other churches—it was quite an interesting smorgasbord! Evangelical Christians, Zen, yoga, spiritualism, the Episcopal Church—we even got involved in a Catholic splinter group which made me their priest. I stayed with them for three years, but their fanaticism finally drove us away.

I decided to give the mainstream Catholic Church one more chance, and enrolled in a master's program at St. Francis Seminary, one of the better Catholic schools in the midwest. There I encountered the same nonsense I had suffered through earlier—only things had gotten worse. Desperately, I concentrated on the psychology courses, thinking perhaps I could use my training later. The seminarians had lost their faith in the divinity of Christ—their faith was in social justice, community action groups, situation ethics, and the thought of Hans Kung!

My wife and I had reached the end of our rope. We prayed on our knees every night for guidance, for some sign of which church to join—much as Joseph Smith had done. We even dared to give the Lord a time limit: one week or we would chuck the whole business of religion!

Apparently, the kingdom of heaven is sometimes taken by force, for two days later, just as we were about to go shopping, the doorbell rang. My wife opened the door to two young men in white shirts and ties, beaming in the July heat. Her face lit up like fireworks: "You're Mormons, right?"

Uncertain of what to do in the face of such enthusiasm, the Elders didn't know whether we were going to hug them or shoot them. We explained our long spiritual sojourn and told them of their providential timing. We went through the discussions like bullets through tissue paper, and were both baptized within two weeks.

It didn't take long for us to discover why the phone had been hung up on us six years earlier. We found out that a Catholic relative staying with the bishop must have answered the phone. The reaction of the vacationing relative was, to say the least, understandable.

Not long after, my wife looked on warmly as Bishop George Warner laid his hands on my head and ordained me to the Aaronic Priesthood. At last I found what I had been seeking— the power of the ordination was so evident that I could hardly stand up from the chair.

It would be nice to say that our lives became a bed of roses after our baptism, but it wouldn't be true. Temporally, our first year as members of the Church was the worst of our lives. I had completed my master's degree, but there was no demand for Mormon teachers of theology in Catholic colleges! Then my wife suffered a severe heart attack and was unable to work, so we were living on my salary as a part-time circulation driver for the *Milwaukee Sentinel.*

Spiritually, however, our lives have been one high after another. Determined to make it to the Salt Lake Temple to be sealed for time and eternity, we succeeded with help from the members. I will not attempt to describe how wonderful this was—suffice it to say that I had never realized how empty our life was until it had been filled.

Since our return from Salt Lake, Alexandria's heart has improved with miraculous speed. In February 1982, the doctors were astonished to report that her heart has almost totally healed. This healing is due to the power of the priesthood.

My wife now teaches in Relief Society, and I, to my humble surprise, have been called as president of the elders quorum. We give many missionary firesides for Catholic investigators. Recently I baptized my first convert—an old friend and former Catholic brother from the Franciscan Order, Frank Chaparas. Like us, he had been seeking for many years the best way to serve the Lord Jesus Christ. He has now found it.

We know that the latter-day gospel is true. That sure knowledge is something only the Holy Spirit can give. No matter how long it takes, it is indeed worth the wait—we testify to that.

A Case of
Mistaken Identity

To meet James Morask is to meet a happy man, although he has been plagued by physical mishaps for most of his life. It was while he was an American Baptist minister and evangelist that Brother Morask started what he felt was the "perfect church." After twenty-two years in the ministry, which included many years of studying the doctrines of The Church of Jesus Christ of Latter-day Saints, he and his wife became members of the Alhambra Ward, Los Angeles East Stake. They have both served as ordinance workers in the Los Angeles Temple.

*L*ife to me has been like an ice cream cone—to enjoy it, I've had to keep licking it. My membership in the Church has helped me to overcome the physical problems which have plagued me off and on for nearly forty years since I suffered an injury during the Battle of the Bulge in World War II. It was in a hospital that I first encountered members of The Church of Jesus Christ of Latter-day Saints, but it would be many years before I would give up my ministry in the Baptist Church to join them.

During my training at the Baptist Bible Institute in Cleveland, I decided to write a master's thesis on contemporary American religions, and I selected Mormonism as one of the topics—nothing could be more contemporary than that! I had heard of the old Mormon temple in nearby Kirtland, so I went over there and knocked on the caretaker's door. As I was walking to the temple with him, he stopped me in the middle of the road and started to explain the differences between the LDS Church and the Reorganized LDS Church (which now owns and maintains the temple). From the way this man spoke, I think he saw me as a theological knight in shining armor who was going to rid the Christian world of the Utah Mormons. Fortunately that hasn't happened.

He then gave me a top-to-bottom tour of the building—the pulleys, the attic, the podium, and every floor and room.

I finished my thesis without ever having met a Mormon in my life. But while I was suffering from an appendicitis attack at the V.A. Hospital in Cincinnati, two young men came up to my bedside. I thought they called me by name, so I said, "Yes?"

"We understand that you would like someone to administer to you," they said.

Although I was a Baptist minister, I had no idea what they were talking about. Obviously it was a case of mistaken identity. Once we got the misunderstanding straightened out we became friends, and we talked theology several times before I left the hospital. I was, however, a little put off when they told me that I had no authority as a minister.

Over the next twenty years, Mormon missionaries often crossed my path, and I took great delight in skinning their theological hides and hanging them on the wall to dry. One of my dastardly tricks was to refer the missionaries to the third chapter of Jude for the answer to whatever scriptural point was under discussion. I delighted at their embarrassment when they quickly turned to Jude to find only one chapter in that book of scripture. In those days I was a "know-it-all," and I had a certificate of ordination to prove it.

However, though I ridiculed the missionaries, I came to understand and believe some of the doctrinal concepts they taught. My personal goal was to establish a "perfect" church, the ideal Christian community, and I later incorporated many of the missionaries' ideas into my own preaching.

I started my "perfect" church at the Liberty Gospel Tabernacle in East Liverpool, Ohio. This town was a hotbed of religious controversy among the "Holiness" and the Nazarene denominations, so there was much curiosity when I advertised for weeks that I was going to start a new and perfect church.

A big crowd showed up to my first sermon, and right in the middle of it a lady jumped up and began speaking in tongues. I knew something about the Pentecostal or charismatic movement, so I waited for her to finish and to hear the interpretation. There was none, so I went on with my sermon.

I soon learned that a group of Mormons had also attended the service to see, in the words of their branch president, the difference between how the Lord organizes a church and how a man (me!) organizes one. After the service the branch president, Kenneth Coombs, came up to talk to me. He posed the question: If the woman had really spoken in tongues, what was the message? Where was the interpretation? He quoted 1 Corinthians 14:27: "If any man speak in an unknown tongue...let one interpret." Brother Coombs invited me to his home to talk more about the gospel of Jesus Christ. At the time I thought he was a local minister, and I had hopes I could convert him and his entire congregation over to my way of thinking. However, I soon found out that he was serving a mission for The Church of Jesus Christ of Latter-day Saints.

Over the next year or so we tried to convert each other. He didn't approach me as other Mormon missionaries had done— instead of raising my ire, he answered my questions. I soon became deeply involved in studying Mormonism, so much so that I was thinking about closing the Liberty Gospel Tabernacle and joining the Church.

But my wife, Marian, was not ready to take that step with me. Over the next fifteen years this would be a recurring problem, although I continued my search for answers about the Mormon Church.

While serving in a Baptist church in Indiana, I worked with a student minister who was a deep thinker. We would often discuss Mormonism back and forth. Then one day he saw a newspaper notice of a large LDS conference to be held in Indianapolis, so we decided we would attend to see what it was like. We went to the church listed in the telephone book, but unfortunately the conference was being held elsewhere. I have often wondered if things would have been different for us had we found the conference.

Having been raised by a Hungarian-speaking grandmother, I resigned from my Indiana congregation when given the chance to take over the pastorate of the largest Hungarian-speaking American Baptist congregation in the United States, located in southern California. When we arrived in the area, we decided to attend an LDS Sunday School before reporting to our new congregation. This meeting was just too different from what we were accustomed to: young boys serving the sacrament instead of adult men; water instead of wine. Besides, the members seemed cold—no one was friendly. This put our investigation of the Church into a refrigerator for a time, but it was only a few weeks before I stopped at a seventies bookstore in my new neighborhood to purchase *A Marvelous Work and a Wonder*. Seldom has a book had such a tremendous impact on me. It has such a ring of truth.

Soon we traveled to Salt Lake City to visit our good friends, the Coombs family. They entertained us very graciously and took us to Temple Square to see a film on the life of Brigham Young. After the film, they bore their testimonies to us, almost pleading that we accept the gospel and be baptized.

I really wanted to. I could envision being baptized in the Tabernacle font which I had just seen, with Alexander Schreiner, Tabernacle organist, playing some majestic piece in the background. But again Marian was not ready, and since I now understood the principle of eternal marriage, I felt I could not join until we could do so together.

So I returned to my congregation. When we undertook a new building project, I volunteered to take a full-time industry job, donating my church salary to the building fund. While I was working at an aircraft plant, a 270-gallon fuel tank fell on me and injured my spinal cord, which in turn led to a progressive nervous degeneration. I was paralyzed from the waist down and confined to a wheelchair.

This condition lasted for several years. Of course I was no longer able to minister to the needs of others, since I was in the hospital so much of the time; however, my health did begin to improve somewhat, although I was still confined to a wheelchair. Some time later I was asked by the executive secretary of the American Baptist Convention if I would be interested in doing some preaching, and since my health was getting better and I had always enjoyed preparing and delivering sermons, I went to the West Hollywood Baptist Church, first as a substitute then later as their minister. But the physical deterioration gradually wrecked my strength, and I became more and more pill-bound. The medications to relieve pain were interfering with my thought processes.

In a way this was a blessing, because I was forced to slow down enough to do some deep thinking about the issues that had been bothering me. I kept a notebook of Bible verses that I couldn't explain by the light of my own church doctrine. I made a note of James's reference to anointing the sick with oil (James 5:14). Another scripture that bothered me was in Matthew 18:18: "Whatsoever ye shall bind on earth shall be bound in heaven." I also noted many references to tithing.

The longer my list of problem scriptures, the harder it was for me in good conscience to preach without referring to the answers I had found in the LDS Church. One of my most popular sermons was about the Savior—and it came right out of the book *Jesus the Christ,* by James E. Talmage.

Finally I realized I couldn't go on receiving a salary from one church while believing in another, so I resigned after twenty-two years in the ministry. I had made my decision to join The Church of Jesus Christ of Latter-day Saints—the only problem was getting Marian to accept what I had to do. When I broke the news to her (and it was really no news at all, since I had been meeting regularly with the missionaries), she agreed under one condition: "I will not let this interfere with the ministry God has given me," she stated emphatically. She was serving at the time as minister of music in the West Hollywood Baptist Church.

But at my baptismal service in February 1971 something happened that changed Marian's thinking. You see, more than anything else I wanted to be physically cured, to walk out of the baptismal font after leaving my wheelchair at the water's edge. I had been praying for this—not so much for myself, but for Marian. I felt she would never join the Church unless the Lord impressed her with something, and I sensed I would be a failure in the Church without her.

Six friends, including two members of the Coombs family, lifted me from my wheelchair into the font. Because I had no control over my legs, they floated to the surface and had to be held down. When I left the water, I tried to step but immediately sank back. I was still unable to stand by myself.

When they lifted me back into my chair, I was very disappointed. Although I was thrilled to be baptized, I had expected a miracle that didn't happen. I felt my faith slipping away, so I asked for a priesthood blessing. As I was receiving that blessing, I tried to remember what it was like to move my toes. Which of my muscles did I use? What was it like to walk? The room became very quiet and still. All of a sudden I could feel my toes moving.

"Let me loose," I said. "I want to walk." Shaking, I shuffled my feet across the floor. It was only a short distance, but two steps would have been enough. I had walked!

Exhausted, I was wheeled into the confirmation service, and there sat Marian. Although she had earlier refused to come, she had had a change of heart. The bishop related what had happened and then asked me to speak. Slowly, I rose from my wheelchair, made my way to the pulpit, spoke, and then returned to the chair. Marian was thrilled to see me regain the use of my legs, and this proved a turning point in her investigation of the Church. After therapy and much physical rejuvenation, five months after my own baptism I was able to enter the font without help and baptize Marian.

I hoped that my physical problems were all behind me, but that was not to be. A few months later, while in Salt Lake City for general conference, I was hospitalized with a form of tuber-culosis that affected my digestive system. A long stay at the Veterans Hospital was required. There I met Elder Mark E. Petersen of the Council of the Twelve. He and his wife, Emma, who had heard of my conversion, often visited me and brought me copies of the *Church News.*

I recovered, but again this was not to be the end of my physical problems. One of the dreams Marian and I had was to work in the temple, and after several years we were called to do that. My health was better than it had been for many years; however, one night when I was returning from the temple I ran into a freeway smashup. The accident drove the bone in my leg into my already deteriorated arthritic hip joint. That put me back into the hospital and into a wheelchair again.

But I am not bitter regarding my health problems. In some Christian philosophies, people are taught to look upon illness or handicaps as punishment. But one of my favorite scriptures says otherwise: "My son, despise not thou the chastening of the Lord, nor faint when thou are rebuked of him: for whom the Lord loveth he chasteneth." (Hebrews 12:5-6.)

I feel I am better off spiritually than ever before. Marian and I both love the Lord, the Church, and each other. My service in the Los Angeles East Stake high council and as communications director for the San Gabriel Valley Region has given me many opportunities to speak about my conversion.

I am very thankful for people like the Coombs family, who had the courage to speak to me and correct my understanding of the scriptures. Because of our friendship with them and the members of the Alhambra Ward, Marian and I are looking forward to many more years of service to the Lord and the Church.

It Felt As If We Had Come Home

Smiling faces on family work charts mounted on refrigerator doors, "steak" houses where no food was served, and a husband that read anti-Mormon literature—these provided the strange combination of events that transformed a chic former nun living in San Francisco to the mother of three and the caring Relief Society president in a midwestern ward.

*T*rain up a child in the way he should go: and when he is old, he will not depart from it" (Proverbs 22:6).

Though my parents are not Latter-day Saints, the standard that exemplifies their life is love of and faith in God, and commitment and service to the Lord. I grew up in a small midwestern community composed primarily of German-Irish Catholics. The parish and school were the focal point of their lives. It was a rare morning that my parents did not start their day at 6:00 A.M. Mass. Daily family rosary together and blessings before and after meals were all just a normal part of the day.

Off to school, we children began the day with Mass, then the school day with "the Morning Offering" (a prayer in which every thought, word, and deed of that day was offered to the Lord), and every class with a prayer. The unparalleled education that I received in that small parochial school from the dedicated Sisters of St. Joseph of Carondelet will forever put Bird Island, Minnesota, on the map for me.

As Catholics, we were taught that God might call us to either the religious life, the married life, or the single state. As a priest, nun, or brother one would dedicate one's life completely to God and the service of His people. In most cases, one who chose the religious life would take the vows of poverty, foregoing the right to own *anything;* of chastity, foregoing the right to marry and have children; and of obedience, following the will of God through obedience to religious superiors and Church leaders.

In the fifth grade, my teacher approached me and asked if I had ever considered becoming a nun, like herself. She felt I might have such a calling and advised me to pray and so live that I might be open to the Lord's desires for me. This sort of counsel was frequently repeated by my teachers in successive years.

When I was about to begin high school, our family moved to Mankato, Minnesota, where I had the good fortune of attending the Academy of Our Lady of Good Counsel, located next to the Motherhouse of the School Sisters of Notre Dame. Though as students we followed a normal high school life, we were aware of the postulants and novices nearby who were preparing themselves for religious life.

A Catholic student organization in which I became very involved was the Sodality of Our Lady. In addition to the daily Mass and prayers all the students were engaged in, Sodalists were challenged to daily spiritual reading, meditation, rosary, and examination of conscience, so as to methodically work toward personal perfection and become more loving and serving towards others. The philosophy and structure of this Sodality for lay people was patterned after that of the Jesuit order of priests. We also happened to have Jesuit priests at our local parish. Through these two influences I grew to admire and identify with the zeal and loyalty to God and the Church that historically have characterized the Jesuits.

With this type of upbringing it was quite natural that I should consider responding to what seemed like the strong possibility of my having a vocation or calling to the religious life.

Strangely enough, I did not choose, as most girls did, an order of nuns near home or with whom I was directly familiar. I located an order, then in southern California, that had been founded in France in the early seventeenth century and lived by a Jesuit Rule, which made it especially appealing to me.

Just one month after my high school graduation my parents and I boarded a plane for Los Angeles, where I was to enter the convent. Our plane had a one-hour layover on the way—ironically, in Salt Lake City. My father suggested we take a cab into town for a quick tour. The cab driver dropped us off on one side of Temple Square and we hiked to the other side, where the cab was waiting to whisk us around the Capitol building and back to the airport. Our brief tour of the Tabernacle and the stories of the pioneers were my first exposure to The Church of Jesus Christ of Latter-day Saints.

For the next two-and-a-half years I was completely isolated from the outside world. Initially I wore the simple black dress, cape, and veil of the postulant. After six months I received the habit of the order: black habit with a white guimpe, black cincture, and rosary and white veil of the novice.

The day started at 5:30 A.M., when we arose, quickly dressed, and gathered in the chapel to chant from the Psalter, meditate for an hour, and attend Mass. We would return to the chapel again to chant the psalms after breakfast, and before lunch, before supper, and before retiring at night. In addition, late in the afternoon we said the rosary and meditated for half an hour. Examination of conscience twice a day kept us constantly evaluating our progress toward self-improvement. In between we had various work and study assignments.

Otherwise we spent the day in silence—always keeping our eyes down and our hands folded in our sleeves as we went from place to place, so that we were not distracted from maintaining an awareness of the presence of God. We did have an hour of recreation when we played ball and could talk after the noon and evening meals, but we never watched TV, listened to the radio, or read a magazine or a newspaper.

This type of life may seem ascetic to some, but I enjoyed the emphasis on a strong spiritual base and can't imagine my life without having had that experience. The culmination of the novitiate was taking the three vows and receiving the crucifix and black veil of the professed nun. Then a Sister embarked on the work of the order or completed her education to do so.

When I entered the convent the Vatican Council was just convening in Rome. When I took my first vows two-and-a-half years later it was well under way. The changes for the Catholic Church in general that resulted from the Council were challenge enough, but added to that, each religious order in the Church was endeavoring to renew itself in light of the Council also.

While many good and necessary things came out of this undertaking, the process was painful and confusing as church leaders and members searched for the appropriate interpretation and application of the new spirit and directives. This was especially so in the Archdiocese of Los Angeles, where I was then attending Immaculate Heart College. Like many other young religious of that time, I found myself questioning this way of life that I had always assumed would be my lifelong pursuit. Disillusioned by the contention and "politicking" that I observed in the Church and in various religious orders, I asked for a release from my vows, only two years after taking them. It took several weeks for this dispensation to come from Rome, and when it did, one of the auxiliary bishops of the Archdiocese wanted to interview me, before signing it, to ascertain why I was leaving. I told him the religious life, as I was experiencing it then, fell short of the Christian community put forth by the Savior. He replied, "Sister, if you think you are ever going to find that, you have stars in your eyes."

I continued with my degree and then took a job teaching high school in Los Angeles. I went to Mass every day and maintained a strong personal prayer life. I tried to teach CCD (catechism) classes at the local parish, but found disagreement between the teachers and the priest. It seemed the harder I tried to stay active in the Catholic Church, the further away I felt. But I had no intentions of leaving it. This church was a part of me, and I loved it. It was ailing at that time. But just as you would not turn away from someone you loved when they are ill, but on the contrary would want to help them regain full health again, so I felt my place was to stand by the Church and be a part of facilitating this time of change.

Just before I was to meet my future husband I received an offer to return to Minnesota and teach at my alma mater. All the arrangements for this had been made when I met Bob on a blind date. Things clicked for us very fast, and I soon found myself driving back to Minnesota with someone else along in the car to introduce to my parents. I did stay to teach one quarter until a replacement could be found. Then Bob returned and we were married in the school chapel, returning then to California to make our home.

Some time before we met, Bob had lived and worked in Salt Lake City, so we stopped off there on our way to California. He showed me Temple Square and told me quite a bit about the Mormons. I could tell he had admired them but that he could not take seriously some of their doctrines. He had become well versed in anti-Mormon literature and enjoyed provoking discussion with it among his aquaintances.

Because of the Mormon concept of eternal marriage which he had shared with me, I had given him as a wedding gift a watch engraved with the words "Yours for time and eternity."

While living in Los Angeles we noticed a Mormon meeting-house next to a Catholic Church we attended one Sunday. Bob suggested we go next door and he would show me what a Mormon Sunday School was like. I'm afraid it pretty much went over my head. The members were friendly and introduced themselves, but I just wasn't ready. Bob referred to the building as a "stake house," and this made me think of a restaurant. Later, we also toured the Los Angeles Temple Visitor's Center, where we saw the film *Man's Search for Happiness*. I remember thinking it was all rather quaint. I certainly did not take it seriously or apply it to myself.

Now that I am a Latter-day Saint I never give up on anyone investigating the restored gospel. Sometimes it takes years for seeds planted to begin to sprout. We never know when our patient efforts will eventually bear fruit. In my case, a series of incidents in quick succession, happening four years later, led to our joining the Church, but our earlier encounters had prepared the ground.

After just a few months in Los Angeles we moved to San Francisco, where I ended up working for the next five years. We had wanted a family but were unsuccessful. However, our days were filled with everything else a newly married couple could dream of: we lived in an exciting city in a charming Victorian apartment; we traveled, entertained, ate out, and enjoyed the cultural life of San Francisco. We found we were not satisfied, though. I was frustrated. We had so much going for us on the surface, but inside I felt empty. I knew why. We needed and wanted children. There was something else too. I had been "trained up in the way I should go," but I had been "departing from it." My spiritual life was flagging, and I wasn't directly involved in service to others.

In connection with my work, I met some Mormon women and was invited into their homes for business meetings. I was impressed with their well-trained children. We had lived in San Francisco for four years and rarely saw families with children — then we would go into these homes and find this burgeoning world reminding me of my childhood. The husbands and wives were in love rather than contemplating divorce, like so many people we knew. Smiling faces decorated work charts on refrigerator doors. We had such a good time with these families.

Soon we found our greatest pleasure was in being with our Mormon friends; they were not as superficial as others we knew. Naturally the question came: "Why don't you come to church with us on Sunday?" One couple were recent converts and we attended their wedding in a suburban LDS chapel. We were struck by the realization that the bishop who officiated was an ordinary individual like ourselves—it had never entered my consciousness before that here was a church that was actually democratic in spirit: no paid clergy, everyone participating and respected equally. The man giving advice to the newlyweds knew what he was talking about from real experience. That made sense to me.

That same month I went to another wedding, of one of my dearest and closest friends from high school. She had also entered a convent shortly after I had, staying about the same length of time but leaving later for her own reasons. After her wedding, she and her husband honeymooned in Tahiti. I was never to see her again, though, for a week later on the return flight she and her husband died as the plane they were on crashed into the ocean. Because our lives had paralleled each other in so many ways, it was like seeing myself die and yet having a second chance to live. I felt compelled to get my life in order and return to the "way I had been trained up" and "should be going."

Shortly after this we entertained our newlywed Mormon friends. Observing my husband's supposed interest in their church, they invited us to the BYU Education Week. Bob was a little put out about it and he declined, but I agreed to go because they had already purchased tickets for us.

Most of the classes I attended were beyond me, dwelling as they did on latter-day scriptures. But one talk given by Brother John Staley, a former Catholic monk, really met me on my own ground. When I read his conversion story in the book entitled *No More Strangers*, I was additionally convinced he was both learned and sincere, and not just some crank. This was the point at which I dropped my defenses regarding the Church. I began to think there just might be something to it, and if there was I had better find out.

I persuaded my husband to come to one of Brother Staley's talks. He too found the man disarming and began to think maybe he ought to read some literature published by the Church instead of all the anti-Mormon material, especially where Joseph Smith was concerned. I too was thirsting for more information. At our request for some literature about the Church, our friends supplied us with a stack of pamphlets about a foot high. I devoured them, reading them every spare minute I had, carrying one or two with me wherever I went. My mind was open. Prior to this, when I read Church literature I would critique it according to what I knew to be true as a Catholic. Now I was ready to be taught by the Spirit. As a Catholic, a major obstacle for me was the Apostasy. The pamphlet "Which Church Is Right?" by Elder Mark E. Petersen was a decisive influence.

After only a few days of immersing myself in such reading I suddenly realized I had gone too far and read too much. I didn't have to be converted—I already was. Much peace came from this, but I didn't want it to cause a problem in my marriage (Bob was still somewhat antagonistic toward the Church), or in my relationship with my family. However, I did not want to procrastinate the redirection of my life either.

My friend's death had brought to my awareness with a jolt that God was supposed to be at the center of my life, with service to others as the natural outgrowth. At home, in Catholic school, and in the convent, this is how it had been. Now I felt I was out in "left field" and had to get back "on track." The Lord's church offered everything I needed and desired.

The following Sunday I said to Bob: "You know that Mormon church that's only a few blocks from us? Let's go over and see what it's like." When we walked into the chapel and joined everyone for the service, we both had a similar feeling, one of finally *coming home.* We felt so right and so at peace that I would have been baptized right then. When the missionaries were introduced to us, I immediately invited them to give us the discussions. I think they were quite taken by surprise, but of course they came to our home the very next night.

My husband was disturbed when he began to see how seriously I was approaching these discussions. I said to him, "You don't have to be baptized now, but I feel I don't have any choice. I know this is right for me." This actually brought on a renewed fervor in Bob for the Catholic Church. He began praying about what he should do. A spiritual experience convinced him that Joseph Smith was a prophet, and soon he too felt he couldn't turn his back on the truth.

As for me, I had never intended to leave the Catholic Church —quite unexpectedly I went beyond it. Here was everything in its fullness, everything I had hoped for and desired for the Catholic Church. I had found the Christian community the Auxiliary Bishop in Los Angeles said did not exist. I felt that the Catholic Church, as much as I loved it, had taken me as far as it could. Now here was something more—the complete package. I would have stunted my spiritual growth had I not reached out for it. We were baptized after completing the six weeks of missionary lessons. A year later our marriage was sealed in the Oakland Temple, on our fifth wedding anniversary.

My parents took the news better than I had expected, though it hurt them. My father felt we were too close as a family for anything to come between us. Unwittingly, I had given them my greatest tribute to their upbringing.

In the nine years since I joined the Church there have been periods of growth, plateaus, and even floundering. This floundering happens when I lose focus, getting so caught up in activity that I fail to examine what I am doing and why. There have been callings in the Young Women, Primary, and Relief Society, work on the welfare farm and on genealogy, along with home and family needs. I have to stop myself in midstream. This leads to an awakening: If I am not remembering Him in all things, as I covenanted at baptism, then how can I expect His Spirit to be with me?

I keep relearning that great lesson taught to me first at home, then in school and in the convent; a vital spiritual life is the foundation and can never be procrastinated. There is much to do, but if prayer, meditation, fasting, scripture study, and journal-keeping aren't a regular part of it, we will be missing the spiritual groundwork of a stable life. The Church can assist us to become perfect, but we must take charge of our own progress.

Currently Bob and I are busy with our two adopted children, and after four years as nursery leader I have recently been called as ward Relief Society president. My various experiences serving in the Church have nurtured my initial testimony that this is a divine work, conceived of by the Lord alone, and guided by him today through a living prophet. Bob and I continue to strive each day to fully dedicate ourselves to Christ and to model our lives after His teachings.

I Wanted Him Perfect

One man's stumbling blocks are another man's stepping-stones. Just ask Norman Knight, former United Methodist minister. Overcoming obstacles seemed to be his forte, especially when it came to investigating The Church of Jesus Christ of Latter-day Saints. Brother Knight is currently manager of the LDS Employment Center in San Diego, California.

*T*he counterfeit nature of Mormonism—what a topic for a sermon! Not only had I chosen a good topic, but after presenting my sermon to my Phoenix United Methodist congregation, I decided my delivery had made it even better.

There was only one problem with the sermon: it was based on misinterpretation, prejudice, and biases, but I didn't know that at the time.

In addition, my ministerial training at Drew University School of Theology left no room for anything but the historical, orthodox, traditional interpretations of scripture and church authority. Any deviation from these time-honored concepts I considered suspect—hence my attack on Mormonism.

It was not easy for me as a Methodist minister to abandon a promising career and embrace a religion I had openly preached against. Many of my old beliefs were hard to topple and wouldn't have fallen at all were it not for a prayerful wife and concerned and patient newfound friends.

My first positive experiences with the LDS Church came after I had invested eleven years in the ministry. After trying pre-medicine and philosophy at Pomona College, I recalled an urge to join the ministry I had felt at a Christian summer youth camp years before. I entered the seminary and was ordained in 1965, after which I served as a pastor in Los Angeles and Phoenix. When I asked for an assignment near the oceanside, we were delighted with a call to La Mesa, California, near San Diego. With my wife, Fran, and our two children, I found a warm and generous 450-member congregation ready to attend to our every need. We were soon wrapped up in marriage-enrichment and youth programs. "It's amazing how wonderful it is here," Fran would say. "It's almost too good: I'm afraid it won't last."

Unfortunately, Fran soon developed breast cancer, which led to her death after thirteen months in La Mesa. We had prayed for her to be healed, but felt it a blessing that she was uncomfortable for only a few days before she died in August 1974. Through it all our congregation loved and cared for us and were just wonderful in our time of need.

In a parent-teacher conference about a year after my wife's death, I was impressed by my daughter's sixth-grade teacher, Vicki. After the meeting I told my daughter I was going to ask her teacher for a date: "Oh, Daddy, don't!" she pleaded. I guess she was afraid I would embarrass her.

Vicki and I had lots of fun together, though I felt like a teenager again—I would sit in my office for half an hour planning a conversation in my mind before picking up the phone to call. Shortly after meeting her I learned that Vicki was an inactive Latter-day Saint; however, that didn't deter me, and soon we were engaged. I assumed that I would be able to lead her into the United Methodist Church, but soon after our marriage I could see that our services didn't seem to feed her spiritually.

We took a delayed honeymoon and spent most of our time fighting about religion, so I encouraged her to go back to her own church. I really believed that upon comparison she would choose Methodism. Since she had been attending church with me, I agreed to attend LDS services with her on an occasional Sunday afternoon.

I came to the Mormon Church with no real knowledge of its teachings—only the few prejudiced ideas I had come across in preparing my sermon years before. I had supposed that Mormons could not be very bright, but I was shocked when I attended my first sacrament meeting in La Mesa. Vicki's bishop was Judge Clifford J. Wallace, and I also met a psychiatrist and a physician, very successful people with whom I could identify and communicate. They certainly were not the bumpkins I had expected to meet. Still, I would come home from the meetings and ask Vicki, "You don't really believe those ideas, do you?"

About this time, Vicki was asked to direct the ward road-show, and you can probably guess who ended up working on the props. Fortunately, another man was assigned to work with me: Duane Huff, the director of the local LDS institute of religion. As we built props for the roadshow, I felt free to ask him questions about doctrine and received more than a few helpful answers. About that time I was invited by one of the members of my Methodist congregation on a week-long cruise, and I took along the standard works to read. After digesting the Doctrine and Covenants, the Pearl of Great Price, and a part of the Book of Mormon, I realized my feelings about the Methodist Church were no longer the same. I came back really disturbed about my role in the ministry.

Until then, I had always felt free to share with my congregation my own religious struggles. However, I didn't feel comfortable about telling my congregation that I was wrestling to know whether the Latter-day Saints or the Methodists had the truth.

Of course, many doctrinal stumbling blocks lay between me and serious consideration of The Church of Jesus Christ of Latter-day Saints. The priesthood ban on Blacks reminded me of the prejudices and conflicts which surrounded me in my childhood, when members of my own church revealed their opposition to the growing black population of my Los Angeles neighborhood.

When I heard on the radio in 1978 of President Spencer W. Kimball's revelation permitting all worthy males to hold the priesthood, I called my institute friend and told him that one of my chief arguments against joining the Church had just been resolved. I was also intrigued at the reaction of the members — their respect for the authoritative voice of the prophet. The role of authority is one of the chief controversies in the Catholic and Protestant communities today, and I was impressed at the contrast.

A second stumbling block—I had never heard of ancient records preserved on metal plates. I was amazed when my friend Duane brought me a four-page pamphlet describing the gold plates of Darius in Persia and the stone box in which they were deposited.

But my chief struggle came in accepting Joseph Smith as a prophet. The tide of negative literature about him bespoke too many faults in his character—he wasn't perfect, and I expected perfection of a prophet. Then I began to think about the times he lived in.

If a man were to declare in our century that he had spoken to God, that he had been given gold plates with new scripture, that all churches were wrong, the entire power structure of the community would turn against him. Joseph Smith was bound to get bad press.

And as I reflected on the troubles and imperfections faced by the prophets of Bible times, I realized I was setting a standard for Joseph Smith that was not a biblical standard. Only Jesus Christ was perfect. As I began to open my mind, the Holy Ghost began to influence me.

While I wrestled with these things, my daughter and I went backpacking with some members of the ward and had a great time. I felt relaxed enough to talk about anything with my new friends, and when I returned I decided to take a leave of absence from the ministry so that I could work things out.

My daughter, who had been attending early-morning seminary, invited me to sit in with her to hear the missionary discussions. My son and I both agreed, and soon some particularly courageous missionaries were sent to us, I'm sure by our Heavenly Father: Elder Kent Maine, raised on a Colorado sheep ranch, and his companion, Elder Mike Stewart.

I remember the night Elder Maine finished teaching the lesson, swallowed deeply, and said: "Brother Knight, I would like you to prepare yourself to be baptized." I told him I appreciated the invitation, but I wasn't ready to do that. We continued to have the Elders over, though, because I enjoyed discussing religion with them—we also enjoyed feeding them!

One evening my wife and I both had colds, so we sent the Elders away when they came. But in the middle of the night we both awoke and looked at each other. I said, "Vicki, I'm tired of fighting it. I know the gospel is true." I had been clinging to the beliefs of a lifetime, but now I knew what I had to do. On Saturday April 7, 1979, I was baptized, and after being ordained a priest I baptized my son and daughter the following Sunday, April 15.

Not long after this I realized the important role Vicki had played in my conversion. She had dropped into inactivity because she had felt so much pressure to get married. As she became more active, after our marriage, she helped me in three ways. First, she never nagged at me to join the Church. Second, she prayed every night that someday I would join (which I didn't know until long afterward). Finally, she would always tell me a little about the lessons after coming home from Relief Society and other meetings. It was a small thing, but it was effective. Those who want to do missionary work should remember Vicki's approach: she had a plan and she prayed patiently.

I now had to make the career transition. My first job after giving up the ministry was in telephone sales; then I worked as a carpenter's helper digging foundations, hauling lumber, and pounding nails. It wasn't easy to trade the social standing of a minister for a job hauling lumber at a job site. Then the recession hit, and I was really in trouble. Out of a job for the first time in my life, I cast around for six months looking for work. Fortunately Vicki had her teaching career, and I was finally able to secure a position managing a satellite store for Deseret Industries. In June 1981 I was hired as manager of the LDS Employment Center in San Diego, a fascinating job which I love very much.

I am grateful for my new understanding. The most influential voice I hear now is that of a prophet speaking with authority. I believe that God gave clear direction to biblical prophets and that he continues today to reveal his secrets through a prophet. Although I believe that Heavenly Father and the Holy Spirit do work in other churches, I am grateful for the gift of the Holy Ghost.

Once I was smugly moving along in the ministry, happy and content in that role, one of the detractors of the LDS Church, those who deny that Mormons are Christians. It is true that our understanding of Jesus is different from that of Christians who characterize themselves as orthodox; but it begs the question to say that "different" means wrong. When I began to look with an open mind, the LDS understanding of the Godhead seemed obviously true and scripturally correct.

I have been asked if I would have joined the Church were it not for Vicki. I probably would not have—but who knows? My congregation was growing and I was pleased, so I just don't know. But overcoming the stumbling blocks has been worthwhile, and I am grateful to say that I am a member of the Church of Jesus Christ.

Three Questions Haunted Me

When Pat McGee calls on Catholics in his role as a stake missionary, he knows how to relate to them. He was a teaching brother in that church for more than ten years, prior to his conversion to The Church of Jesus Christ of Latter-day Saints in 1976.

What a difference five years can make! In 1971 I was a teaching brother in the Catholic Church, plagued by three fundamental questions about the faith I professed and taught. Then, in 1976, I was baptized a Mormon, my questions answered and a new quest before me: perfection and exaltation in the celestial kingdom.

I cannot recall at just what point in my ten years of college, religious studies, teaching, and pastoral work these questions began to trouble me. Though I had been taught all my life that the Catholic Church was true and I was willing to accept that with an act of faith, I needed to resolve the problems that caused me such unrest.

First, I was vaguely disturbed at the lack of continuity between the church of the Testaments and the Roman Catholic

Church of the twentieth century. The scriptural Church in its simplicity was bound to the Lord by covenant and directed by prophets. The Catholic Church, on the other hand, had grown into a complex medieval power structure, its teachings and practices bearing little resemblance to the church described in the scriptures and the writings of the early Fathers.

To shore up my faith, I told myself that sometime, somehow, the Lord himself would eventually restore the truth and make things right again. But two more questions still festered in my mind.

I could see that the ancient Church was guided by divine revelation. The Lord revealed his will to the prophets, who in turn taught the truth to all who would listen, sometimes in the face of open rebellion. Many, particularly the Apostles under the leadership of Peter, gave their life's blood in testimony to that truth. However, the Catholic Church taught that revelation died with the last of the Apostles, that all divine truth had been revealed before that time and is now to be maintained by tradition.

It seemed to me, however, that much Catholic doctrine and practice had evolved after revelation had ceased. If so, the church was teaching man's ideas, not God's. But how could this be? Again, I tried to withhold judgment—sometime the Lord would resolve this under his immediate direction.

But a third question still haunted me—one that could not be put aside like the others. The church taught the necessity of infant baptism, that all men are born under original sin and must be cleansed by baptism at birth or relegated for eternity to "limbo" (defined as "the abode of souls—as of unbaptized infants—barred from heaven through no fault of their own"). Such infants and the families they leave so soon were generally refused the consolation of a Catholic funeral and burial in a Catholic cemetery.

As I pondered this, I could not reconcile it with the all-just, all-loving God I had come to know and love as my Father. How could God hold a tiny infant responsible for something he did not do? And to what purpose then was the eternal atonement of Jesus Christ? The question demanded an adequate answer, and the ones I was given just didn't make sense. I felt that no father could act in such a way toward a child of his own. I could not accept all I was told to accept, but I couldn't just leave the Catholic Church. I could, however, leave the full-time religious life— which I did in 1971.

Soon I was on my own, living and teaching in Yuba City, a northern California community. My life was enjoyable and challenging—even exciting—but my unsolved questions still seethed. Then, late one summer, the school district sent me to Salt Lake City to study a new reading program at a week-long seminar held across the street from Temple Square.

One evening I took a walk through the Square and went back to my motel room reflecting on the many times in the past I had come in contact with the LDS Church. I had once done a college research paper on the pioneer movement, and had always been impressed with Mormon houses of worship I had seen. But my response was noncommittal—I was a Catholic, and I had faith that the Lord would eventually resolve my inner conflicts.

That fall I found myself working part-time for the reading program I had studied in Salt Lake. This work took me around the country, often with other staff members who were Mormons. We discussed gospel topics in the evenings, but I could not bring myself to believe that I was hearing the truth I sought.

Then, on May 21, 1976, word spread around the Yuba City campus that our choir's bus had been in an accident. Bit by bit the news of the tragedy filtered in—one teacher and twenty-eight students had been killed. The entire community was in shock, and I called the local priest to volunteer whatever help I could to the grieving families.

His response surprised me: "You must not have been a Catholic very long." When I asked him what he meant, he explained that Catholics do not generally go to their priests for that kind of help in their times of need.

Patrick McGee

On Sunday I visited the family of a Mormon girl who had been killed. Though they were not Mormons, they had been touched by the care and concern shown them by the members of their daughter's church. The next morning, I attended a funeral in the Yuba City Ward chapel for five LDS girls. The building was packed, and loudspeakers carried the service to others who filled the grounds. I was deeply moved. I came away from that service with a perspective changed by the intensity of feeling, both physical and spiritual. This was something I had to find out more about.

With the end of the school year, I moved to Salt Lake for six weeks on my reading project and boarded with the family of my future wife. Here I began to study the LDS Church more carefully. When I returned home, I knew what I had to do. I sent to a university for some books containing the writings of early church Fathers; I wanted to investigate the Great Apostasy the Mormons speak of and perhaps resolve the first two of my three questions. While waiting for the books to arrive, I received a copy of the August 1976 *Ensign* from my future mother-in-law.

In Salt Lake, I had told her how much I liked the hymn "O My Father," and this issue contained a pictorial essay about the hymn. But more importantly, I also found an article entitled, "The Apostles and the Apostasy." I read and reread this article into the early morning hours, and finally I knew that it was time to go to my knees. I was intellectually convinced that The Church of Jesus Christ of Latter-day Saints was what it claimed to be—the true church of Christ. I needed spiritual confirmation, however, and as I knelt there seeking a divine witness to what I had learned, my prayer was answered. I knew without a doubt that the LDS Church was true. I had also found the answers to the three questions that had plagued me for years.

I was now ready to be baptized, but I postponed my baptism in response to my mother's request that I discuss it in depth with her first. The day of that conversation is forever burned into my memory—it was a most painful day for all of us. As I left the home where I had grown up, I began to understand the full meaning of the Lord's apparently harsh comment: "He that loveth father or mother more than me is not worthy of me" (Matthew 10:37). But I had a testimony of the restored gospel and knew that in spite of the misunderstanding with my family, all would be well. I was baptized on October 9, 1976, in the Salt Lake Granite Park Stake Center.

Often as I reflect on my conversion to the Church, I realize that it was a journey that covered the greater part of my life. The Church touched my life in many small ways. I remember the buildings—the Los Angeles Temple near my childhood home; the local ward meetinghouse in Yuba City; the East Brunswick Stake Center in New Jersey, near a good friend's home; the Washington Temple; and Temple Square in Salt Lake City. But mostly I recall the people I encountered—the pioneers I researched; the two friends who grew up next door to me; the students I taught in Yuba City, who taught me much about the Church, often without ever saying a word; the reading staff with whom I worked; the family members who were to become my in-laws—all these taught me by both word and example. In each case I can see the loving hand of an Eternal Father guiding his son into the light of the truth.

A year after my baptism, I received my endowment in the Salt Lake Temple as well as further confirmation of the rightness of my decision. Early the next day, I returned to that temple with Edy Adams, the one I love, to be sealed for time and all eternity. In the years since, we have been tried, but also very much blessed, particularly in the arrival of our two children. We are excited to grow as a family, sharing our lives on earth and anticipating all that is to come.

The Church of Jesus Christ of Latter-day Saints is true. It was restored to the earth by the Lord's direction through the Prophet Joseph Smith after years of apostate darkness. In the Restoration I find the same simplicity as in the Church of the Old and New

Testaments, as well as the very well-spring of living revelation. We are conditionally promised not only salvation but also exaltation in the highest realms of the celestial kingdom, where our Eternal Father rules and reigns forever. To this I solemnly testify in the sacred name of Jesus Christ, Amen.